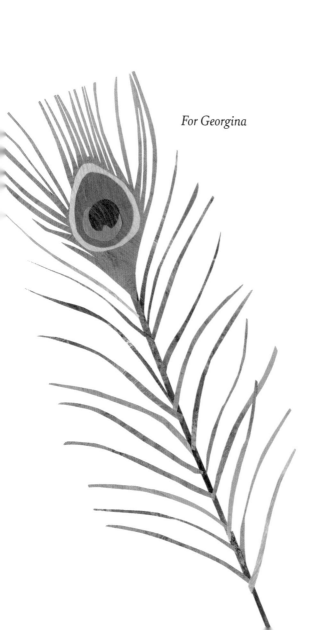

For Georgina

Bird Lore

The Myths, Magic and Folklore of Birds

Sally Coulthard

Illustrations by Clover Robin

Quadrille

Contents

Introduction

Our close relationship with birds goes back tens of thousands of years. We have long relied on birds for food and feathers but perhaps, more importantly, early societies also looked to the skies with awe and envy. Birds could do so many things we longed to emulate. Virtuoso melodies, soaring flight, razor-sharp eyesight and brilliant plumage – birds had it all.

It's perhaps no surprise, therefore, that many of our earliest cultural experiences were infused with birds. From cave paintings to feathered costumes, we have constantly tried to capture birds' qualities in our music, dress and art. One of the world's earliest flutes, for example, was carved from the wing bone of a vulture 40,000 years ago, while it was an owl that our Stone Age forebears patiently carved into the soft rock at Chauvet-Pont-d'Arc in France around 30,000 BCE. More recently, it has been birds that inspired some of our greatest poets, composers and writers to pen their masterpieces.

Over the centuries, we have also done birds a great disservice. Many a bird's undeserved reputation was fabricated by a Latin scribe or medieval monk, scribbling away in an ivory tower. Fowlers and farmers long persecuted birds, often for completely misguided reasons. Explorers greedily grabbed the prettiest specimens and sailed them back home, starting a cruel craze for caged exotic birds. And even the most promising physicians believed birds could cure strange, intractable ailments or entice someone to magically fall in love.

Bird lore – the myths, magic and language of birds – still resonates today. Summer swallows, festive robins, Easter chicks and snow geese – every season has its bird emblem. We pepper our sentences with avian words and expressions such as 'ruffled feathers', 'feeling broody', 'night owl' and 'up with the larks'. Both children and adults alike enjoy tales about birds, many of which have their roots in ancient fables and cosmologies. From wise old owls to ugly ducklings, blue jays to mockingbirds, it seems every avian has a story to tell.

Robin

*Nothing in the world is quite as adorably lovely as a robin
when he shows off – and they are nearly always doing it.*

FRANCES HODGSON BURNETT: *THE SECRET GARDEN* (1911)

Few birds are as universally esteemed as the robin. For centuries, gardeners,
poets and writers have regarded this dainty bird with huge affection. 'His gentle,
pleasing manners' enthused Victorian naturalist Robert Fletcher, 'his winter song,
his confiding trust in man and his readiness to accept hospitality all combine
to make the robin an especial favourite'. We see the best of ourselves in its
confident, cheerful companionship. Shakespeare famously called it 'charitable',
Chaucer admired it for being 'tame', and Wordsworth dearly loved the robin, his
'pious bird with the scarlet breast'.

The robin's rouged feathers became its calling card. The Anglo-Saxons called
it the *ruddoc*, or 'red thing', the Elizabethans the 'redbreast'. In many European
languages, the robin is defined by its bright coat – *rouge-gorge* in French, *pettirosso*
in Italian and *roodborst* in Dutch. For centuries, Christian folklore imagined the
robin's ruddy chest came from the Crucifixion, drops of Christ's blood forever
staining the bird's feathers as it fluttered to help. This association with soothing
the dying also expressed itself in the belief that robins covered the bodies
of the unburied with moss and greenery, an act of sacred devotion.

The sixteenth-century ballad *Babes in the Wood* revealed the robin hard at work:

> *No burial this pretty pair,*
> *From any man receives,*
> *Till robin redbreast, piously,*
> *Did cover them with leaves.*

Reverence for the robin also protected it from much of the casual cruelty often inflicted on other birds. Many superstitions focused on the misfortune that would haunt those who harmed 'God's own bird' or its nest. Anyone foolish enough to kill a redbreast invited all manner of troubles, from spoiled milk to being struck by lightning. Even a cat who caught and ate a robin was thought to risk losing a paw.

Robins are, of course, also a cherished symbol of Christmas. This may have its roots in the nineteenth century, when postmen wore red uniforms and were nicknamed 'robins'. These red-breasted delivery men soon became linked to the novel Victorian craze for sending cards during the festive period. More likely, however, is that robins and winter celebrations have an older association. The robin is one of the few garden birds to stay put during winter, its song a rare seasonal melody. As one eighteenth-century tale rejoiced: 'when all the rest of the feathered tribe are silent grown, the robin red-breast [...] will often perch and sing his Christmas carol to the jolly rustic, huddled around his fire, and drinking down his horn of wholesome ale.'

When early English settlers began to colonize the New World, they applied the name 'robin' to any bird that bore a loose resemblance. Of the more than a hundred 'robins' that are now found from Australia to America few are closely related to the original robin redbreast. But that doesn't make any of them any less beloved.

Owl

In the North, people consider the cry of an owl as strange and frightening, and they all dislike it.

LIU XUN (9TH CENTURY CE)

Throughout human history, the owl has represented a contradiction. In many cultures, the bird was both a worrying omen and a sign of wisdom, a dichotomy that often revealed itself in myths and legends. In medieval bestiaries – compendiums of real and imaginary animals – owls were often pilloried as birds of the night, ghostly animals that preferred to swoop among graveyards and gloomy caves. Our limited understanding of their nocturnal behaviours also led to strange beliefs about owls flying backwards, being lazy or polluting their own nests. Liu Xun, writing in ninth-century China, described the owl as not only a bringer of bad luck but, worst still, 'unfilial' because it reputedly showed no loyalty to its parents.

In European culture, an owl's cries were said to mark the loss of a maiden's virginity or the death of a loved one. Edmund Spenser called it 'The messenger of death, the ghastly Owle' in his sixteenth-century work *The Faerie Queene*, a sentiment echoed in Shakespeare's *Macbeth*. When Lady Macbeth hears Duncan murdered, she cries: 'Hark! Peace! It was the owl that shrieked, the fatal bellman, Which gives the sternest good night.' In early Welsh mythology, Blodeuedd – a beautiful woman fashioned from flowers – was unfaithful to her husband and conspired to kill him. Her attempt failed and as punishment she was transformed into an owl; a bird – according to the legend – hated by all other avians.

Yet not every belief about the owl was so unkind. In Greek mythology, an owl was the close companion of Athena, goddess of wisdom, warfare and protector of Athens, and Minerva, her Roman equivalent. Athena's owl represented her foresight and lethal strategy, qualities much admired in the Greco-Roman world. These ancient beliefs were thought to have been rooted in even older traditions, inherited from the earliest civilizations. Many nascent cultures believed in some form of mother goddess, the embodiment of life and death, light and dark. The owl, both a hunter and an inhabitant of the night, represented one half of this cosmology. In Celtic mythology, for example, the Cailleach was an old woman, the creator goddess. The *cailleach-oidhche*, or owl, was the 'crone of the night'.

For some cultures, the owl was an envoy between the worlds of the living and dead, or the incarnation of a spirit. Muut, for instance, was the messenger of death for the Cahuilla people of southern California and northern Mexico, and was usually depicted as an owl who escorted newly deceased souls to the afterlife. In Mayan culture, four owls acted as emissaries between the underworld, Xibalba, and the human realm. In Inuit society, the owl was a wise guide, safely ushering wandering spirits to their final resting place. The owl was also held in huge regard by the Lakota people of Dakota, especially when it came to the mystical insights required for healing ceremonies. Medicine men were believed to obtain their magical abilities during the night, through dreams as clear and focused as the owl's sight. Wisely, anyone who harmed an owl would lose this precious power forever.

Pheasant

I will place the Pheasant, as being indeed a
Byrd of singular beauty, excellent in the pleasure of her
flight, and as rare as any Byrd whatsoever that flies.

GERVASE MARKHAM (1655)

For a bird so closely associated with the British countryside, the pheasant is
a deeply exotic import. Long domesticated across Europe, its name comes from
the ancient Greek *phasianos* or 'Phasian bird'. The City of Phasis, now lost to
archaeology, was thought to be a busy trading port located somewhere on the
east coast of the Black Sea. Phasis raised and exported pheasants for the Greek
table, a trading relationship captured in a caustic epigram from the time: 'Neither
mullet, Baeticus, nor turtle-dove delights you; nor is hare ever acceptable to you,
or wild boar. Nor do sweetmeats please you, or slices of cake; nor for you does
Libya or Phasis send its birds.'

It was a prized game bird throughout the Greek and Roman periods,
three times as expensive as the peacock. A handful of birds' bones from
Romano-British sites suggest the Romans may have imported the pheasant
into Britain, although evidence for a resident breeding population is scant.
For such a now-ubiquitous bird, the pheasant was until Victorian times, a bit
of a rarity. One mid-eighteenth-century book of ornithology, *A New General
History of Birds*, described the pheasant as a 'fine *Fowl* [...] very much esteem'd
here in *England*, not only for its Scarcity but the fine Taste of its Flesh.'

The English may have loved the pheasant for its culinary appeal, but its handsome appearance didn't go unnoticed: 'The Colours of the Head look very Beautiful', the ornithological volume continued, 'and the shades have a Delightful Appearance from the Reflection of the Sun.' Other cultures had also long appreciated the startling beauty of the bird. In Japanese folklore, the pheasant was considered a messenger from heaven. Texts from as early as the seventh century compared cosmic auroras to dazzling red pheasant feathers, stretched across the sky. In 1947, the green pheasant or *kiji* was declared Japan's national bird.

In China, the pheasant is considered an emblem of good fortune. The mythical Chinese phoenix is said to have the head of a pheasant, the legs of a crane and the feathers of a duck (see page 123), and is thought to appear at moments of great joy and peace. The pheasant is also associated with bravery. In ancient times, Chinese officials wore a military cap decorated with pheasant feathers, known as a *wuguan*. Male pheasants were observed fighting, sometimes to the death, during the mating season, battles that became synonymous with martial victory and valour. This tradition can still be seen today in Chinese opera, where long, elegant pheasant tail feathers, or *lingzi*, are attached to helmets and hats, especially those belonging to heroic or military characters.

Puffin

There is also a kind of fish called a Puffin [...] a Syren or mermayden.

THOMAS COGAN (1636)

For centuries, the puffin belonged to the sea. It seemed as at home under the waves as it did soaring above rocky outcrops, and was regarded as a hybrid – part bird, part aquatic creature. Elizabethan playwright Thomas Nashe called it 'halfe fish, halfe flesh', while a century later monks even persuaded the Catholic Church to allow puffins to be cooked and eaten on Lent days. Holy fasting forbade the consumption of meat and poultry but the brothers, who 'cried fish not fowl', persuaded not only Church physicians but also the archbishop that the puffin should be included within the dietary laws.

The name puffin literally means 'puffed up with air' or 'swollen' and, since medieval times, was applied to a least two different but similar looking fat nestlings. These were baby Manx shearwaters and true pufflings (baby puffins), both of which were sadly caught and eaten. Nowadays, only true puffins retain their chubby moniker.

For much of the year puffins live out in the open ocean, from the east coast of Canada to northern Russia, but in springtime head to the cliffs of remote islands and coastal stretches. Well into the late nineteenth century, marginal fishing communities on places such as the Faroe Islands and Outer Hebrides often relied on the bird for food, although puffins weren't to everyone's taste. Writing in 1785 ornithologist John Latham in his *A General Synopsis of Birds* noted, with some disgust, that 'they are excessively rank, yet the young are preserved with spices, and pickled, and by some people much admired.' He added the rather gruesome footnote that they 'Are potted in St Kilda and elsewhere and sent to London as rarities. The bones are taken out, and the flesh wrapped in the skin; are eaten with vinegar and taste like baked herring.' Puffins are also Lundy Island's most famous bird. The name 'Lundy' comes from the Viking or Old Norse *lundi*, meaning puffin, an ancient place name that can also be found in Lundey, Iceland.

For a bird now regarded with enormous affection, the puffin was once a symbol of buffoonery. Early portrayals of the bird often described it as clumsy or ungainly. Known by its folk name, the 'Clown of the Sea', the collective noun for puffins was also a 'circus' or an 'improbability'. Other names were gentler, inspired by the puffin's distinctive features. Some called it the 'sea parrot', others a 'coulter neb', after its plough-like beak. The scientific name for the puffin is *fratercula*, or 'friar', after its black-and-white monastic feathers, and the Cornish called them 'popes'. Similarly, in Iceland the nickname for puffins is *prófastur* or priest. Scottish islanders, however, loved the shy puffin's natural reserve and called the bird the 'tammie norrie' or 'Tom Noddy', a name also applied to a bashful, awkward suitor.

Chicken

The wind took off with the sunset
The fog came up with the tide,
When the Witch of the North took an Egg-shell
With a little Blue Devil inside.

RUDYARD KIPLING (1919)

The myths and meanings surrounding the chicken have long been linked to its sex. While the cockerel symbolized traditional male traits such as bravery and aggression, the hen became shorthand for motherhood and docility.

Both the Greeks and Romans loved cockerels for their fighting prowess, a skill that was seen as both necessary and glorious. For these ancient civilizations, the cockerel represented everything a warrior should strive to be – fearless, combative and full of pride. The ancient Greek for cockerel, *alektor*, meant 'defender from evil', a word that still lives on in alektorophobia, the fear of chickens.

The Romans also believed in Mercury, a deity who acted as a mediator between gods and mortals, and escorted dead souls to the afterlife. Mercury was said to be born at dawn, the boundary between night and day, and many statues and representations of Mercury featured his companion – a cockerel – a bird who announced dawn, the day's rebirth, with his glorious crowing. This symbolism is also echoed in Christian teachings – Jesus predicted that Peter would betray him before

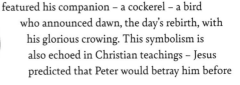

the cock crowed the following morning. Peter did, but soon repented, and dedicated his life to spreading the Christian message. In the ninth century, the cockerel became Peter's emblem, a sign of spiritual reawakening and the power of light to banish darkness. Many church spires are still crowned with cockerel weather vanes to this day.

The symbolism of the hen, however, couldn't be more different. Eggs, hens and women's power have long been linked in Western culture. Witches were commonly said to have hens as familiars, creatures who would do dastardly deeds on their behalf. Witches were also thought to sail in hen's eggshells, bobbing along the water in these tiny craft. While empty shells had the potential for malicious magic, the uncracked hen's egg represented rebirth and life's potential. Many societies' early myths, from China to Tahiti, West Africa to Finland, have 'cosmic eggs' in their origin stories where universes or gods hatched into the world. The egg is also central to ideas about Jesus' resurrection in orthodox Greek, Russian and Slavic versions of Christianity.

Folkloric tales often link hens and eggs to ideas about rebirth and fertility. English superstitions and practices, for example, would sometimes involve 'oomancy', the art of fortune-telling using egg white dropped into water, while on St Agnes' Eve unmarried women were encouraged to eat an eggshell before bed so they could dream of their future husband. After their winter break, hens were also expected to start laying again on Valentine's Day, a sign that spring's fertility had returned:

> *By Valentine's Day,*
> *all good hen, duck or goose should lay.*
> *By David [1 March] and Chad [2 March],*
> *every hen, duck and goose should lay, good or bad.*

Woodpecker

While the Nightingale warbled and quaver'd so fine,
That they all clapp'd their wings and declar'd it divine!
The Skylark, in ecstasy, sang from a cloud,
And Chanticleer crow'd, and the Yaffil laugh'd loud.

ANON (19TH CENTURY)

The Romans revered the woodpecker. In the great founding myth of Rome
the twins Romulus and Remus were protected by a she-wolf and fed by a kindly
woodpecker who, according to Greek biographer Plutarch, 'visited them and,
perching near on tiptoe, would, with its claw, open the mouth of each child
in turn and place therein a morsel, sharing with them a portion of its own
food.' Roman philosophers were impressed by the woodpecker's industry and
determination. Pliny the Elder called it a 'courageous and spirited bird that has
a beak so strong it can overturn oaks by pecking them', and marked it sacred to
Mars, the god of war.

The ancients also believed the woodpecker had magical powers. Birds'
behaviours were watched closely and interpreted as either good or bad
omens. If a woodpecker landed near you, it was seen as deeply auspicious.
If a woodpecker witnessed you picking peonies, however, it would try to peck
your eyes out. One of the strangest beliefs from the time involved a species of
woodpecker called a 'wryneck', which gets its name from its ability to turn its
head almost 180 degrees. The Greek name for the wryneck was the *iynx* and it
was a bird often used in love spells. A wryneck would be tied, spreadeagle, to a
small spinning wheel, while a charm was recited in the hope it would bring back
an unfaithful lover. Such was the popularly of this erotic ritual that terracotta or

metal models of woodpeckers on spinning wheels eventually substituted the real thing. Over time, the word *iynx* became jinx, a word we still use to describe an unlucky enchantment. Body parts of a different species, the black woodpecker, were also carried as amulets to deter harm from leeches and bees.

The mystical power ascribed to various species of woodpecker continued through the Middle Ages and beyond. The green woodpecker was colloquially known as the rain bird or rain fowl, as its cry was thought to predict a downpour. The green woodpecker was also the 'hew-hole' (*hew* means to cut or chop), while the great spotted woodpecker was known as the 'specht' or 'speight'. The noun, now lost, remains a popular surname, especially in northern England. Originally Anglo-Saxon, it would have been given to a person whose characteristics were thought to match those of a woodpecker, perhaps because they were talkative. Interestingly, the green woodpecker was also known as the 'yaffil', 'yaffle', 'yaffingale' or 'yuccle', after its distinctive call. In Scots, one of the native languages of Scotland, the word 'yaff' is still used to describe a yelp or bark, or someone who's a chatterbox.

Flamingo

Truly to admiration when I viewed this Creature, I have been led into speculations to contemplate the Creations.

JOHN POYNTZ (1683)

Six species of flamingo live across the world. While four have made their home in the Americas, another two have flocked to the shallow lakes of Africa, Asia and southern Europe. Early zoologists couldn't quite decide whether the flamingo was a magnificent type of crane or a lowly goose (see page 30). As the writer and natural historian Oliver Goldsmith penned in the late seventeenth century, 'The flamingo has the justest right to be placed among the cranes; and tho' it happens to be webbed footed, like birds of the goose kind, yet its height, figure and appetites, entirely remove it from that grovelling class of animals.'

All who saw the flamingo first hand, however, were dazzled by its extraordinary colour and body shape. With its pink torso atop pencil-thin legs, such an eccentric and flamboyant bird only served to strengthen observers' faith in God's creativity and 'manifold works'. Maritime adventurers and Christian missionaries often returned with wonderful tales of flocks of flamingos in their natural habitats. Colonists also found the birds unusually fearless around human beings, a habit soon exploited. Goldsmith noted that 'When Europeans first came to America, and coasted down the African shores, they found flamingos [...] on either continent, gentle, and no way distrustful of mankind.' In no time at all, however, Western firearms and an appetite for fowling soon turned the trustingly tame flamingo into one of the 'shyest birds in the world and most difficult to approach'.

The flamingo appears in hieroglyphics, and one sign denotes both the bird and the colour red, although little is explicitly said about the creature in Egyptian mythology. Many other cultures also named the bird after its fiery colouring. The ancient Greeks called the flamingo *phoinikopteros* or 'red-wing', and Aristophanes praised it as 'very handsome with his wings as crimson as flame'. Even its modern name, flamingo, is thought to derive from the Latin *flamma* or flame. The Italians call the flamingo *fenicottero* (crimson feather) and the French, *flamant rose* (flaming pink). In Hindi, flamingos are *agnipankh* (wings of fire); in China they are the *huo-lie-niao* (the 'fire-intense bird').

The Nivaclé people of Paraguay, however, tell the best story about how the flamingo got his colouring. A woodpecker (see page 22) decided to attack the King Buzzard. As he pecked, violently, under the buzzard's wing, the bird of prey began to bleed. All the other birds went to help, throwing the woodpecker aside but getting covered in blood in the process. The buzzard's blood made all the birds itch, so they quickly washed it off. Only two birds didn't mind the spill and loved their vibrant new colour. One was the spoonbill. The other was the flamingo.

Ostrich

I'll make thee eat iron like an ostrich,
and swallow my sword like a great pin.

WILLIAM SHAKESPEARE (1594)

In the luxuriously illustrated pages of the *Queen Mary Psalter*, a fourteenth-century book of psalms, there is a very unusual drawing. A medieval peasant is bending down, on one knee, and feeding horseshoes and nails to an ostrich. The idea that ostriches loved to eat strange objects had been around for a least a thousand years before this date. Pliny the Elder, in the first century CE, had written with confidence that ostriches were 'able to digest every substance without distinction', an idea further developed by thirteenth-century monk Vincent of Beauvais who emphatically affirmed that 'the great bird ate and digested iron'. Some medieval families even used the myth to their advantage. In Scotland's fifteenth-century coat-of-arms guide, the *Deidis of Armorie*, one heraldic crest shows an ostrich eating an iron key. Anyone bearing this sign, explains the book, isn't to be messed with. Beware anyone who 'eite hard thingis' and was 'diffailland [defiant] of natur'.

Few medieval chroniclers would have seen an ostrich, a bird native to the savannahs of Africa, in real life. But that didn't stop authors describing the creature with vivid and often totally inaccurate detail. As well as its eccentric appetite, the ostrich was said to throw rocks with its camel-like toes. Indeed, the Greeks called the ostrich the *strouthokamelos*, or camel-sparrow, an animal deemed neither bird nor totally mammalian.

27

In the Bible the ostrich was also branded a terrible mother who abandoned her eggs and ill-treated her offspring. Early Christian teachings used the ostrich to demonstrate the idea that looks can be deceiving. The ostrich may have great wings adorned with beautiful feathers, but it cannot fly. Everything, therefore, is not always as it seems. Ostriches are also, erroneously, said to bury their heads in the sand in fear, a behaviour that became shorthand for stupidity and cowardice.

Thankfully, one civilization recognized the true magnificence of the ostrich. In ancient Egypt, ostriches were an important symbol and often associated with the concept of *maat*, or truth, balance and justice. Maat was also a goddess who represented these ideals, and always wore an ostrich feather. The Egyptians believed that at death a person's heart was weighed to see if their good deeds outweighed the bad. If the deceased had led a virtuous life, their heart would weigh less than Maat's feather and a place in paradise was assured.

Ostrich eggs were prized by the Egyptians, their broken fragments fashioned into beads for jewellery. But they weren't the first to do it. Ostrich eggshell beads had been used to cement relationships between hunter-gatherers in Africa for thousands of years. Recent archaeological discoveries in Lesotho, in southern Africa, reveal ostrich jewellery was used as a prehistoric social currency over 30,000 years ago. Hunter-gatherer groups, more than 1,000 kilometres (620 miles) apart, are thought to have swapped ostrich beads as a way of creating friendships and forging alliances across vast, unimaginable distances.

Goose

*One might almost be tempted to think that these creatures have
an appreciation of wisdom [...] one of them was the constant companion
of the philosopher, Lacydes, and would never leave him, either
in public or when at the bath, by night or by day.*

PLINY THE ELDER (1ST CENTURY CE)

The Exeter Book was written late in the tenth century. It's one of the great jewels
of English literature. Alongside its haunting pages of Anglo-Saxon poetry there
are also about a hundred riddles, including 'What Am I?':

'My beak was close fettered, the currents of ocean running cold beneath me.
There I grew in the sea, my body close to the moving wood. I was alive when
I came from the water clad all in black, but part of me white. When the living
air lifted me up, the wind from the wave bore me afar.'

The answer is, bizarrely, a goose. Or a barnacle goose to be more precise.
For centuries, people believed that this beautiful black-and-white species
had grown from barnacles and limpets knocked off the bottom of sailing
ships. Others thought barnacle geese grew on trees over water;
the goslings would hang from their beaks until they
were old enough to let go.

Unlike many other species of geese, barnacles breed and raise their young out of sight in the Arctic, an absence that no doubt led to the confusion. The habits of domestic geese, however, were better known. Geese played a major role in village life, not just for meat and eggs, but also for fat and feathers. They were said to be able to smell intruders from far away and were often praised as protectors and companions, fierce and unfailingly loyal. In Rome's fledgling years, a sacred flock of geese was kept in the Temple of Juno. When the Gauls tried to storm the city in the early fourth century BCE, while the guard dogs snoozed, the holy geese honked furiously and saved Rome from disaster. Every year thereafter, the Romans both praised geese and punished dogs. In the *supplicia canum* – the 'punishment of the dogs' – the failure of the guard dogs to bark was marked by the ritual crucifixion of canines; at the same time flocks of geese were decorated with lavish fabrics and paraded with pride.

In many parts of eastern Europe and Scandinavia, goose is traditionally served on St Martin's Day (11 November). Legend has it that, in the fourth century, St Martin was so unwilling to be made a bishop that he hid in a barn full of geese, but his location was given away by their noisy squawking. Only 400 years earlier, however, Caesar famously wrote that the Celts ate neither goose, nor hare nor cockerel (see page 20), all of which were believed to be sacred. The Egyptians also revered the goose: Gengen Wer, the celestial 'Great Honker', was said to guard the cosmic egg from which all life emerged.

Ptarmigan

I'll hunt the roe, the hart, the doe, The tarmigan sae shy, lassie.

ANON (19TH CENTURY)

The ptarmigan is a bird of extraordinary resilience. The word applies to three different species of partridge-like grouse, all of whom eke out an existence on the planet's harshest terrain. Ptarmigans live in the coldest, least-inhabited regions of the globe, including frozen mountains, Arctic forests and barren tundra. They are also brilliantly camouflaged and change, like ice-bound chameleons, from snow-white winter plumage to earthy, grey-brown summer feathers.

Their Latin family name, *lagopus*, means 'hare-footed'. Ptarmigans are unusual in having toes covered in stiff feathers, a quirk noted by Pliny the Elder in the first century CE. Subsequent translations of Pliny's work, however, resulted in some strange errors. Of the ptarmigan, the thirteenth-century monk Thomas of Cantimpré declared that these strange birds could only eat in secret, hiding inside caves, and that when a ptarmigan died its body magically withered away because it had lived such a meagre existence. He also claimed they couldn't fly, which also isn't true. Other natural historians made blunders about the bird, too. Its name comes from the Scottish Gaelic *tàrmachan*, meaning 'bird that murmurs or croaks', but in 1684 Scottish antiquarian Robert Sibbald added a silent 'p' to the front of the word, wrongly believing it to have originated from the Greek *pteron* – 'wing'.

The ptarmigan is famously shy and Victorian writers loved the romance of the bird's isolated existence. The peace and solitude of the Scottish Highlands, one of the ptarmigan's strongholds, appealed to those for whom the pleasures of industrial urban life had worn thin. 'It is delightful to wander far from the haunts', wrote one world-weary naturalist, 'and ascend the steep mountain, seat one's self on the ruinous cairn that crowns its summit, where, amid the grey stones, the Ptarmigan gleans its alpine food. There, communing with his own heart, in the wilderness'.

In Japan, the ptarmigan is known as *rai-cho,* or 'thunder-bird', and is regarded as sacred to the god of thunder, who is also thought to live in the mountains. Images of the ptarmigan were often hung up as lucky charms in rural cottages, as protection against extreme weather. In the northern regions of North America, the ptarmigan was hunted as an important source of seasonal game but the bird also held ritual significance. In Tlingit households in southeast Alaska, for example, ptarmigan feet would be rubbed on a newborn's face so the baby would grow up to be as nimble and quick as the flighty bird. The ptarmigan's feathered feet were also said to have inspired the earliest Tlingit ancestors to create snowshoes. For the Inuit, male hunters were sometimes divided into 'ptarmigans' and 'pintail ducks', depending on whether they were born in winter or summer respectively. Duels, dances and tugs of war between the two groups were arranged to predict success in the following season's hunts.

Raven

...the Raven [...] is aware of all the births, baptisms, marriages, death-beds, and funerals. Often does he flap his wings against door and window of hut, when the wretch within is in extremity, or sitting on the heather roof croaks horror into the dying dream.

CHRISTOPHER NORTH (1842)

The raven was, indisputably, the bird of the dead. Ravens are carrion eaters, nature's recyclers of flesh and fur. Through the centuries, different cultures have been both fascinated and repulsed by how these intelligent, resourceful creatures would appear at an animal's dying moments, whether a lamb in the field or a warrior on a bloodied battlefield.

In Celtic myth, warfare had its own goddesses – the *Morringán* and the *Badbh*. These battle-furies were shapeshifters, who changed from women to ravens, and haunted the arena of war. Not only would their attendance presage a violent death, but these craven crones were also thought to interfere in disputes, stoking tensions and encouraging slaughter. And once the fighting was finished, these dark divinities would transform into ravens and pick over the flesh of the fallen.

While ravens no doubt prophesied death for the pugnacious Celts, they were also a symbol of aggressive, merciless warfare and much admired. The collective noun for ravens is still an 'unkindness'. Ravens appear on Celtic artefacts and coins, including a remarkable helmet adorned with a metal raven. Found in Romania, and dated to the third century BCE, the raven's wings were hinged, and would have flapped terrifyingly as the warrior raced into combat.

The raven was also special to another battle-hardened culture: the Vikings. In Nordic mythology, Odin famously had two ravens – *Huginn* (Thought) and *Muninn* (Memory), who were sent out to the ends of the Earth to return in the evening with important news. Ravens were also seen as symbols of divine but brutal justice; ancient Norse poetry calls upon the raven to exact retribution, pecking out the eyes or tearing at the hearts of the unworthy or lawless.

For the Tlingit people of the Pacific Northwest coast of North America, however, the raven wasn't a bird of death or retribution. Instead, it perfectly embodied our capacities and foibles. Seen as neither good nor bad, the raven was thought to mirror the human experience, the constant tug between self-sufficiency and greed, wisdom and hubris. The raven was also a creative cheat whose cunning provided humans with the foundations of life – the sun, moon, stars, fire and fresh water. A similar, thieving raven creation god – *Kutkh* – belonged to a number of indigenous groups in Russia and north Asia. For them, the raven was both a trickster and the ancestor of all humankind.

Cuckoo

Sumer is i-comen in.
Groweth seed and bloweth meed
And springth the wude nu.
Sing cuccu!

SUMMER CANON (13TH CENTURY)

Of the approximately 150 different species of cuckoo, about 60 raise their young in an extraordinary way. Known as 'brood parasitism', the female cuckoo lays her egg in another bird's nest. The unwitting surrogate then raises the egg as her own, not realizing the error even when the cuckoo chick looks markedly different from her own. Far from getting along with its siblings, the baby cuckoo also kills the other chicks or shoves the remaining eggs out of the nest.

Such egregious, cunning behaviour has long intrigued naturalists. As early as the fourth century BCE, Aristotle had spotted the cuckoo's fostering out of her chicks. He believed the cuckoo was such a timid parent and so unable to defend her young that she cowardly placed them under the protection of another species. In reality, brood parasitism is a ferociously successful evolutionary strategy; freeing a parent from chick-raising duties allows it more time to forage and lay more eggs.

Medieval writers thought the female cuckoo not only left her offspring in the care of others but also constantly and lustily swapped partners. Fourteenth-century knight and poet Sir John Clanvowe called it 'That sory brid, the lewde cukkow'. Indeed, the cuckoo's deception inspired another ancient word – 'cuckold'

– meaning the husband of an adulteress. The idea of women's sexuality and faithlessness in a marriage allowed cuckold to become not just a comic phrase, but a scandalous slur. Shakespeare's *Othello*, for example, violently boasted to Iago on learning of his wife's supposed infidelity: 'I will chop her into messes! Cuckold me!'

The cuckoo's distinctive voice certainly attracted attention. Early versions of its name – *cuccu*, *cokkow*, *kukkowe* and eventually, *cuckow* – copied the bird's two-note call. Folklore and superstitions centred on hearing the cuckoo's first call of the year, a sure sign that spring had returned. Victorian rural labourers, especially in Shropshire and Lincolnshire, would celebrate hearing the first cuckoo with the joyous quaffing of cuckoo-ale. Counting the number of the spring cuckoo's calls would also tell you how many years before you wed or, more worryingly, died. In countryside circles, the proverb 'Cuckoo oats and woodcock hay, make a farmer run away' referred to a spring so unseasonably cold that oats couldn't be sown until the first cuckoo was heard.

A strange frothy liquid also appears on certain plants with the arrival of the spring cuckoo. Cuckoo-spit is created by an insect called a froghopper. In Irish folklore it was said that the tiny bug inside the cuckoo-spit was the last thing the cuckoo ate before migrating for winter. When the cuckoo returned the following spring, she had to spit out the same bug before she could sing, leaving small piles of foamy saliva on young shoots of plants.

Canary

Now tell me, little songster,
You toil not, neither spin,
What bringeth thee such happiness
In your little house so trim?

'But I am always happy,
In cage though I'm confined,
And sing to show my gratitude
Whenever I'm inclined.'

MARY A. BUCHAM (1905)

The Canary Islands sit off the northwest coast of Africa. For centuries, explorers and traders coveted this wildlife-rich archipelago, but one bird in particular caught their eye. The canary, a particularly pretty finch, enchanted sailors with its melodious singing and soon found itself smuggled back to Spanish shores in the sixteenth century. These small, affable birds bred easily in captivity and other European countries soon caught on to the craze. By the nineteenth century, canaries were an immensely popular pet among the gentry and working classes alike.

People delighted in the canary's beautiful singing voice and gentle, biddable temperament. The canary was also thought to be permanently content, despite its caged confines. Victorian society saw in the canary something about the domestic ideal, especially the role of women in the middle-class household. Both the canary, and the wife, should be 'blithe and airy', a beautiful and charming attendant who enjoys being restricted to the domestic sphere. Canary manuals

praised the bird as a simple, breezy 'companion and entertainer of children and invalids', while Robert L. Wallace in his 1893 *The Canary Book* expanded on their appeal: 'there is no more an engaging bird than the canary; nor any more gay, happy and cheerful in confinement'. Ironically, most people kept male canaries, as the females tended not to sing.

The canary, as the ultimate 'pet of the parlour', was also employed as a teaching metaphor in religious sermons and children's books. Taming a bird, and removing its wild nature, created a placid, genial creature suitable for polite society and was seen as an instructive lesson for children, unmarried women, the poor and degenerate. Spending time with a canary would, according to one Victorian bird-keeping manual, help people learn about 'love, kindness and patience' and reclaim them from the 'haunts of vice and crime'.

In stark contrast to the overstuffed confines of a middle-class living room, canaries were also famously kept by miners. In the late nineteenth century, British physician John Scott Haldane proposed taking canaries into coal mines to act as an early-warning signal to detect carbon monoxide. The birds, who were more sensitive to the toxic gases than the miners, would exhibit distress at the first sign of a leak, allowing miners the chance to escape. The phrase 'canary in a coal mine' is still used to mean an early warning sign of danger.

Magpie

Fortune of empires often hung
On the magician Magpie's tongue...

CHARLES CHURCHILL (1763)

The name 'magpie' is fascinating. The 'pie' bit is thought to come from the ancient word *peyk*, meaning point or pick, no doubt a reference to the magpie's piercing beak. For centuries magpies were often known simply as 'pies' but, during the medieval period, the addition of 'mag' added an extra flourish. Shakespeare referred to 'magot pies' in *Macbeth* (1623), Randle Cotgrave the 'magatapie' (1611), while Samuel Pepys wrote of the 'magpyes' (1666). Despite the differences in spelling, it seems 'mag' was a contraction of Margaret or Marguerite, a name unkindly used to mean a woman who talked too much or gossiped.

From Roman times, magpies were viewed as intelligent communicators. Pliny the Elder, writing in the first century CE, thought the magpie a gifted mimic, who could not only repeat human words but also ponder their meaning. If a magpie struggled to articulate a particular word, insisted Pliny, it would need to hear it repeatedly until it could copy it exactly. If the magpie couldn't grasp the word, even after these efforts, it would die of frustration. Early medieval scribes also praised the magpie's ability to imitate human speech. According to the *Aberdeen Bestiary*, a twelfth-century book of beasts, 'Magpies are like poets, because they utter words, with a distinct sound, like men; hanging in the branches of trees, they chatter rudely, and even if they cannot get their tongues round words'.

Magpies were also thought to be prophetic birds. Many ancient civilizations looked to the avian world for divination – their proximity to the sky-gods, ability to defy gravity and strange calls would have all held meaning. The magpie, with its human-like voice, would have attracted particular interest, as Shakespeare alludes to in *Macbeth*:

> *Augurs, and understood relations, have*
> *By magot-pies, and choughs, and rooks brought forth*
> *The secret'st man of blood.*

In Christianized Europe, the appearance of a magpie was almost always seen as bad luck – 'Whan pyes chatter upon a house it is a sygne of ryghte evyll tydynges'. Rural sayings also dipped into this superstition. Many people still know the 'One for sorrow, two for joy' doggerel although many different regional versions exist. Seeing a solitary magpie was also bad luck and required the observer to act out a counter-charm, such as saluting the magpie or enquiring after his wife. Countryside beliefs also focused on the magpie's reputation for thievery – we still use the phrase 'magpie' to describe someone who collects and hoards shiny objects.

Not all cultures eyed the magpie with suspicion, however. In China, magpies are often depicted in pairs and are still seen as messengers of love and joy, especially on the Chinese version of Valentine's Day. The Qixi Festival celebrates the reunion of a mythical couple – the Cowherd and the Weaver Girl – when a flock of magpies formed a bridge with their wings, allowing the two lovers to reunite.

Lark

Yet in those thoughts myself almost despising,
Haply I think on thee, and then my state,
Like to the lark at break of day arising
From sullen earth, sings hymns at heaven's gate;

WILLIAM SHAKESPEARE (1609)

The lark represents spontaneous joy. Almost all English poetry about this perching bird celebrates its carefree, seemingly limitless flight and cheerful chatter. Shakespeare chose it as the perfect bird for his sonnet, the lark as both subject and metaphor for the power of love to lift despair. Milton too admired the lark for its ability to bring happiness from darkness:

To hear the lark begin his flight,
And singing, startle the dull night...

Indeed, many poets saw themselves in the lark and envied its freedom and self-expression. Nineteenth-century poet Francis Thompson admired the lark's clear, unaffected voice: 'Does the skylark, singing sweet and clear, Beg the cold world to hear?', while William Wordsworth called it 'Ethereal minstrel! Pilgrim of the sky!' Shelley longed to be as adept as the lark – 'Poet hidden, In the light of thought' – and saw the bird as having a creative, uninhibited spirit.

George Meredith's 1907 poem *The Lark Ascending* inspired composer Vaughan Williams to write a movement by the same name, a musical work that captured the rising song of the lark, delivered as it soared skyward:

> *As up he wings the spiral stair,*
> *A song of light, and pierces air*
> *With fountain ardor, fountain play,*
> *To reach the shining tops of day...*

The heights to which the lark could reach, and its habit of singing at the break of dawn, also appealed to the religious. Medieval scholars wrote about the lark and its habit of flying aloft, seven times a day, to sing hymns to God. Larks were said to trill at heaven's gate, being harbingers of the new day, and became synonymous with early risers; we still use 'larks' to describe morning people. The lark's job was also to rouse the indolent from their slumber, so they could start the day's labours and say their morning prayers, or 'Matins'. As seventeenth-century poet Robert Herrick penned in *To The Lark*:

> *Good speed, for I this day*
> *Betimes my Mattens say:*
> *Because I doe*
> *Begin to wooe:*
> *Sweet singing Lark,*
> *Be thou the Clark,*
> *And know thy when*
> *To say, Amen.*

One ancient Greek fable, which also has Indian, Arabic and African parallels, centres on the lark. The bird was said to have been created even before the Earth was formed; when her father died, the lark had nowhere to bury him because there was no ground. And so, she made a grave inside her own head, the burial mound creating the lark's familiar crest. The moral of the story is that a child's first duty is reverence to their parents.

Dove

Lizzie heard a voice like voice of doves
Cooing all together:
They sounded kind and full of loves
In the pleasant weather.

CHRISTINA ROSSETTI (1862)

While the dove is now a universal symbol of peace, it started life as the bird of love and female sexuality. In ancient Mesopotamia, now present-day Iraq, doves were the symbol of Inanna, a formidable goddess. Inanna, also known as Ishtar, was the deity of sensuality, warrior power and procreation, and was often believed to take the form of a dove or have one as a companion. Successive civilizations, influenced by the idea of Ishtar, also developed the link between doves and fertility deities. In ancient Greece, sacred doves were sacrificed at the Aphrodisia, the main festival to celebrate Aphrodite, goddess of love and lust, while small white dove figurines were offered at her temple in Daphni. Rome's Aphrodite equivalent, Venus, was also associated with doves, who were said to pull her chariot across the skies. This myth was still being referenced over a thousand years later in a line from Shakespeare's *Venus and Adonis*: 'Two strengthless doves will draw me through the sky'.

Shakespeare's sonnet also mentions 'two silver doves that sit a-billing', a beautiful metaphor that might explain the bird's ancient association with love. 'A-billing' described doves rubbing their beaks together, which many interpreted as kissing. Doves also appear to 'marry' in monogamous pairs and both parents take assiduous care of their young. Their gentle trilling and cooing also seems strangely human, like intimate pillow talk between lovers, a notion alluded to in Christina Rossetti's nineteenth-century sensuous poem, *Goblin Market*. In it, two sisters are tempted by seductive, dangerous fruit offered by enchanted sprites.

In the Christian canon, however, the dove has a different meaning. In the Bible, at Jesus's baptism, we read: 'And straightway coming up out of the water, he saw the heavens opened, and the Spirit like a dove descending upon him: and there came a voice from heaven'. For thousands of years, both doves and pigeons (which belong to the same bird family) were used as messengers – birds were said to convey the names of winners at the Olympic Games across ancient Greece. The symbol of the dove as holy messenger also appears in the myth of Noah's Ark. In the story, Noah – who has been at sea for over a month – sends out a dove to find evidence of land. The dove returns, bringing an olive branch in its beak, both of which have become potent symbols of salvation and new spiritual beginnings. In 1949, after the horrors of war, Picasso famously created *La Colombe*, or 'Dove of Peace', a black-and-white lithograph used on the poster for the Paris Peace Congress later that year. The dove has been an iconic symbol of world peace ever since.

EGGS

It's hard to imagine an object more perfect than an egg. Unbroken, unblemished and full of potential, the egg has, for many cultures, been used as a key motif in religion, folklore and cosmology (explanations of how the universe was formed).

The egg's miraculous biology – where life seems to spring magically from dormancy – has also helped it to become a metaphor for reincarnation, rebirth and new beginnings. In Greek mythology, for example, Chronos, the god of time, created a cosmic egg. Out of this origin egg hatched Phanes, the god of life, who brought light and formed the world. Similarly, in Tahitian cosmology, the creator Ta'aroa began life inside an egg, which he broke his way out of. Part of the egg became the sky while Ta'aroa himself became the Earth.

Folklore, which often focuses on everyday items and household routines, has plenty to say about the egg. In English superstition, for instance, witches were thought to shrink and sail across rivers or seas in hens' eggshells, and to use empty eggshells for brewing mischievous potions; many people would therefore smash eggshells once their contents were eaten. Eggs also feature in love magic, perhaps because of their intimate association with ideas about birth and fertility. One form of divination, called oomancy, involved 'scrying'; reading the patterns of albumen when floated in water. Eating a hard-boiled egg before bedtime, its empty yolk filled with salt, was also thought to entice a young woman to dream of her future lover.

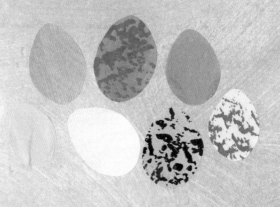

Hoopoe

As nasty as a hoopoe.

PROVERB (18TH CENTURY)

For a creature as regal looking as the hoopoe, with its crested crown, it has long been regarded as a dirty inferior. In fact, looking back through descriptions of this magnificent avian in Western texts, it's difficult to find someone with anything nice to say. Aristotle, writing in the fourth century BCE, insisted the hoopoe made its nest out of human excrement, and the idea was expanded a millennium later by Isidore of Seville. For him, the hoopoe slept on human waste and fed on foul dung. 'It is a most loathsome bird', he sniped, 'always dwelling in tombs and human muck.' If that wasn't bad enough, Isidore added a final damning flourish: 'Anyone who anoints himself with the blood of this bird and then goes to sleep will see demons suffocating him.' Ninth-century monk Rabanus was no less scathing in his assessment. For him, the hoopoe symbolized wicked sinners; 'men who continually delight in the filth of sins'.

The poor old hoopoe had, it seems, been dreadfully misunderstood. Scholars' obsession with faeces comes from a peculiar defence mechanism employed by the bird. The female hoopoe has a special gland that produces a tremendously smelly secretion. The bird rubs these foul-odoured juices over its body, to waterproof its feathers and protect them from bacteria. When the female hoopoe is nesting, this gland goes into overdrive and produces enough unctuous liquid to also cover her eggs, providing the shells with an extra layer of antibacterial protection. Hoopoe chicks also quickly learn their own method of self-defence once hatched; if threatened, nestlings will squirt a well-aimed jet of faeces directly at an intruder.

Not everyone agrees on why the hoopoe is so called. The standard etymology is that 'hoopoe' comes from the Latin *upupa*, a word that mimics the bird's repetitive calls of 'hu-poo-poo'. It's interesting, however, that the French words for 'hoopoe' and 'crested' are very similar – *huppe* and *huppé* respectively. Ancient author, Varro, tells a gripping tale of why the hoopoe's cries sound like they do. In Greek mythology, Tereus was the deeply unpleasant king of Thrace. He raped his wife's sister and so, in revenge, his wife killed their own child and served up the boy's flesh at the dinner table. On discovering what he had just eaten, and wracked with horrified grief, Tereus was transformed into a hoopoe. The hoopoe's calls are the king's never-ending cries for his lost son – *pou pou* in Greek translates to 'where where?'

Thank goodness, then, for the Persians, who saw the hoopoe as a symbol of virtue and connection. In *The Conference of the Birds*, a poem composed in the twelfth century, the hoopoe is both a loyal envoy and leader of all the other birds:

> *Dear hoopoe, welcome! You will be our guide:*
> *It was on you King Solomon relied*
> *To carry secret messages between*
> *His court and distant Sheba's lovely queen.*
> *He knew your language and you knew his heart.*

Toucan

*The most extraordinary part of these birds is the enormous
beak [...] of gigantic dimensions, seeming big enough to give
its owner a perpetual headache.*

JOHN GEORGE WOOD (1862)

When European countries first set their greedy eyes on South America, in the Age of Discovery, they had gold and glory on their minds. What they soon discovered, however, was a tropical landscape full of natural riches more dazzling and diverse than anything they had ever seen. And one of the most spectacular creatures they encountered was the toucan.

Explorers couldn't believe their eyes. The French adventurer Jean de Léry, in his *History of a Voyage to the Land of Brazil*, published in 1578, noticed how prized the toucan was among indigenous tribes. Toucan feathers were used for ritual dances, ceremonial dress and even facial decoration. Small, yellow feathered patches were dried and glued to each side of the face: 'These yellow plaques, worn on their cheeks', he noted, 'seem like two ornaments of gilded copper on the ends of the bit of a horse's bridle'. Indeed, in many native South American cultures, toucan feathers were widely used in ritual clothing, especially by shamans hoping to emulate the toucan's qualities or gain their spiritual strength. Headdresses were often constructed with rows of feathers that mirrored birds' ecological niches in the forest – eagles and other high-flying birds' feathers at the top of the headdress, toucan feathers in the middle and the ground-dwelling curassow's at the bottom.

Not only does the toucan have brilliantly coloured feathers but it also has a most remarkable beak. Léry was also one of the first writers to describe the toucan's outsized bill: 'The beak of this bird, the toucan, which is longer than the whole body and proportionately thick, must be regarded not only as the beak of beaks, but also as the most prodigious and monstrous that can be found among all the birds in the universe.' Other early writers called the toucan the 'Bird All-Bill' or the 'Grosbeak'.

No one, however, could work out what the beak was *for*. Georges-Louis Leclerc, Comte de Buffon, one of the eighteenth century's most admired nature writers, called the toucan's bill one of 'nature's errors' and compared it to one of 'those long-nosed masks that frightens children'. Some scholars believed the large beak was designed to seize fish from the river or hollow out trees like a woodpecker, despite the fact that no one had ever seen a toucan do either. Or, that the toucan was so heavy and gluttonous that its bill evolved so it could reach and devour huge mouthfuls of fruit while remaining seated. More recent research, however, has shown a fascinating alternative, that the large surface area of the toucan's bill allows it to regulate its body temperature in the heat of the rainforest.

The name toucan is thought to come from *tuka* or *tukana*, words in the Tupí-Guaraní languages once spoken by the native people of Brazil. What it means, however, isn't quite certain. While some etymologists believe the word imitates the toucan's cries, others think it may have originally meant 'feather' or 'nose bone'.

Nightingale

*A poet is a nightingale, who sits in darkness and sings to cheer
its own solitude with sweet sounds; his auditors are as men entranced
by the melody of an unseen musician, who feel that they
are moved and softened, yet know not whence or why.*

PERCY BYSSHE SHELLEY (1840)

Few birds are as poetic as the nightingale. Shelley compared the act of writing verse to a nightingale trilling into the evening. The bird sings its beguiling song without any consideration of an audience but still the performance is both intimate and revealing.

One of the earliest connections between poetry and the nightingale was made over 2,000 years ago. The *Palatine Anthology*, a collection of ancient Greek verse from the seventh century BCE, revealed how Stesichorus the poet was given his lyrical gifts as a newborn baby: 'at his birth, when he had just reached the light of day, a nightingale, travelling through the air from somewhere or other, perched unnoticed on his lips and struck up her clear song.' Two millennia later, in the spring of 1819, the nightingale was still inspiring great works. John Keats' much-loved *Ode to a Nightingale* was written under a plum tree in the London garden of a good friend. A nightingale had built a nest nearby and Keats was said to have experienced a 'tranquil and continual joy in her song' and felt moved to put pen to paper.

Not all the nightingale's associations, however, were so innocent. *The Owl and the Nightingale*, a medieval poem about a fierce debate between the titular birds, shows a darker, more erotic connotation. In it the nightingale is criticized by the owl for being a bird who only sings in summer, a time when all of nature is aflame with sexual desire. 'And you are like them yourself, because your song is all about lechery [...] As soon as you've mated, you lose your voice, and instead chirp like a titmouse, squeaking hoarsely'. The nightingale's nocturnal associations also added fuel to this salacious interpretation. Chaucer played on the erotic double meaning in his *Canterbury Tales*: the squire 'loved so hotly that till dawn grew pale, He slept as little as a nightingale.'

In Persian folklore and literature, the nightingale and the rose were deeply intertwined. The nightingale was said to be maddened by love, and could neither eat nor sleep, and would channel its sexual longing by singing towards the roses. In Persian mysticism the rose also represented divine perfection; the nightingale, the fallible human lover. Together, the rose and the nightingale symbolized these opposing roles – the beautiful, proud and sometimes cruel beloved, and the endlessly devoted follower. Spiritual interpretations of the nightingale's yearnings saw the rose as a metaphor for the soul's desire to unite with God.

Myna

An' I swagger an' scold an' strut an' I swagger,
An' pick up me fun where I can,
Or tell off me wife, who's a bit of a nagger,
Or scrap with the sparrers for scran.
A bonzer at bluffin', I give you my word,
For, between you an' me, I'm a pretty tough bird.

C.J. DENNIS: *THE INDIAN MYNA* **(1935)**

The myna, native to Asia, is a chatty, sociable bird with a ferocious intellect. It is also a brilliant mimic. People have long been mesmerized by the bird's ability to repeat the human voice, a skill that resulted in myna birds frequently trapped in cages or kept as house companions. Writing at the end of the nineteenth century, nature and travel writer John Madden was captivated by what he regarded as the 'very best talking pet' while visiting Calcutta. There, in the Great Eastern Hotel, 'Every morning with daylight it would begin in a gruff male voice: "Boy! Bring me some wine!" presently it would change to "Waiter! Bring some water!!" in a lady's voice – or again, "Good morning, Gentlemen!"'. Another author, E. F. Hutchinson, on an extended stay in Peshawar during the 1880s, wrote a wonderfully evocative account for *The Globe* newspaper: 'One of my birds caught the cry of my child so perfectly its grandmother would toddle about the house after the suffering little one. Another coughed to perfection, but became vulgar by learning to expectorate, and a third sneezed admirably'.

Asia, however, didn't need telling what a wonderful bird the myna was. For thousands of years, many of its nations had praised the bird for its human voice and devoted courtship. The name myna comes from the Hindi *mainā*, which in turn derives from the Sanskrit *madanā* meaning 'joyful or delightful'. In ancient Sanskrit texts, one species – the hill myna – was called the 'love arrow' or 'love dart'. Hill myna birds were taught by professional trainers to recite endearing phrases or *bon mots* to please their royal owners, especially those birds that were kept in palace harems. Other caged hill mynas were taught to repeat religious or moralistic phrases. As myna birds tend to mate for life, they were also associated with love and companionship; in Nepalese culture, the myna bird is seen as a symbol of undying love and, with its partner, the parakeet (see page 135), was thought to be half of a devoted couple.

In India, seeing a pair of myna birds is considered lucky, although one alone, like a magpie (see page 43), is inauspicious. A rich and colourful folktale from India tells the fable of the peacock and myna, and why we should be wary of flattery. Both birds agreed to a dancing match. The peacock, with its then-pretty feet, danced beautifully. The myna, spying an opportunity, appealed to the peacock's vanity and asked if they could swap feet so the myna might dance as well as the peacock. The peacock agreed but the myna fled, taking the peacock's handsome feet with it. The peacock still dances elegantly to this day but, when it looks down at its now-ugly feet, it weeps bitterly, reminded of its conceited folly.

Curlew

Wild as the scream of the curlew,
From crag to crag the signal flew.

SIR WALTER SCOTT (1810)

In 1467, to celebrate the inauguration of the new Archbishop of York, over 18,000 birds of various shapes and sizes were served to guests, including cranes, egrets, peacocks (see page 97), bitterns (see page 79), herons and curlews. Curlews were once a prized game bird, and expensive, at three times the cost of a woodcock. This premium came not from their rarity, but from the fact that curlews were only palatable for half the year. During summer, curlews lived on moorland and meadows but over winter they migrated to the salty shorelines and estuaries, turning their flesh strongly fishy. Fowlers knew the monetary value of the seasonal curlew and even had their own proverb: 'A curlew lean or a curlew fat, Carries a twelve pence on her back.'

The most ravishing thing about the curlew, however, is its voice. Its calls are high-pitched, but strangely human, like a whistling cry; its harmonies beautifully melancholic. In the Old English poem *The Seafarer*, about a man lost on the waves, the curlew's shrieks remind him of how isolated he is:

> *...the voice of the curlew,*
> *instead of the laughter of men,*
> *the singing gull,*
> *instead of the drinking of mead.*

In the early twentieth century, William Henry Hudson, one of the RSPB's earliest supporters, wrote exquisite prose about the curlew, sensing its decline in the landscape as a result of senseless egg collecting and hunting. For him, the curlew had an 'inflected wild cry', that 'wild yet human-like whistle it uttered in my hearing was its last farewell'.

The curlew's distinctive rising call was so haunting that some even connected it with death or bad weather. In both British and Irish folklore the legend of the Seven Whistlers tells of a group of eerie spirit birds who fly at night, and whose unearthly cries warned of a forthcoming disaster. Sailors were also particularly wary of curlew cries, which were believed to predict a terrible storm. Writing in the 1930s, journalist Sir Charles Igglesden recorded fishermen's superstitions: 'I knew we were in trouble when the Seven Whistlers flew over us with their "ewe-ewe" cry. Our men wanted to turn back. The night came on with wind and rain, and sure enough before the morning a boat was capsized and seven poor fellows drowned. I never did like those birds.'

The curlew also holds deathly associations among some Indigenous Australian peoples. The Noonuccal tell a story of how curlews are the guardians of the dead and carry their souls to the sky world. Among the Wardaman people, the night-calls of the curlew are a forewarning of dire news. And, for the Tiwi of Melville Island, the curlew is the spirit of Wai-ai, the wife of creator god Purukupali. The cries of the curlew are Wai-ai wailing with remorse at the death of her baby son.

Albatross

And as them birds went sailing by
Something about them caught my eye
And as I gazed I grew surprised
For both of them I recognised.

FRANK WATERS, *ALBATROSS* (1927)

The albatross was, undoubtedly, the sailors' bird. Both spent long, lonely weeks at sea, coming ashore only briefly, and seemed kindred spirits. These vast ocean birds, with impressive sail-like wings, followed vessels for days without resting. Sailors often held these birds in superstitious awe; albatrosses were sometimes said to be the souls of dead mariners. Carl Linneaus, the father of modern taxonomy, gave the albatross the Latin name *Diomedea*, after the Greek warrior Diomedes whose companions were also turned into birds.

Herman Melville, author of *Moby-Dick* published in 1851, wondered if the albatross's magical allure might come from the angelic colour of its plumage: 'Bethink thee of the albatross', he wrote, 'whence come those clouds of spiritual wonderment and pale dread, in which that white phantom sails in all imaginations'. He was also thrilled by its 'uttered cries, as some king's ghost in supernatural distress'.

Perhaps the most famous literary work about the albatross is, of course, *The Rime of the Ancient Mariner* by Samuel Taylor Coleridge, first published in 1798. A mariner and his shipmates, on a ship trapped in the ice near the South Pole, are visited by an albatross. The crew view the great bird as a lucky sign and, sure enough, the ship soon breaks free and sails away. The albatross accompanies the ship further on its journey but in a moment of random folly, the mariner shoots and kills the bird, placing a curse onto the entire crew. We never learn why the seaman shoots the bird, but his anguish is only relieved when he learns

to love all the creatures of the sea: 'For the dear God, who loveth us, He made and loveth all'. The poem was a huge hit and, for many, an allegory about sin and redemption.

The poem also, unwittingly, created the myth that sailors never killed albatrosses for fear of bad luck. In reality, seamen have been catching and eating albatrosses since the beginning of long-distance navigation. In the 1590s, on his travels around the South Seas, Sir Richard Hawkins described hooking an albatross with a piece of bait on a fishing line, a technique continued through the centuries. Others were shot and eaten. Joseph Banks, on Captain Cook's *Endeavour*, wrote that in February 1770 the albatrosses were so delicious everyone 'eat heartily of them tho there was fresh pork on the table'. Even Ernest Shackleton, the great polar explorer, regularly turned to albatross meat on his gruelling missions. Indeed, in one entry he mentioned the fateful poem of the ancient mariner: 'we sympathise with him', he mused with typical pragmaticism, 'but wonder why he did not eat the albatross, as it would have made a very welcome addition to his larder.'

Blackbird

The fourth day of Christmas,
My true love sent to me
Four colly birds
Three French hens
Two turtle doves, and
A partridge in a pear tree.

ANON (18TH CENTURY)

When we sing *The Twelve Days of Christmas* with festive gusto few of us know that we're singing the wrong words. 'Four calling birds' was originally 'Four colly birds' in the earliest printed version of the seasonal verse, in a 1780 children's book called *Mirth Without Mischief*. 'Cole' or 'coal' is a word with a fabulously ancient pedigree and one that appears across much of Europe in different forms. From the Viking *kol* to the early German *kula*, it was used to describe both the fuel and the colour black. Colly, therefore, meant black or soot coloured, like the outside of a kettle, and was the perfect name for one of our most recognizable garden birds. In some parts of southwest England, the blackbird is still known as the colly.

Indeed, blackbirds appear in another famous children's rhyme – *Sing a Song of Sixpence*. The familiar lyrics were first printed in the 1700s but the practice of putting songbirds in pies was well established by the fifteenth century. One Italian cookbook from around 1400 – *Anonimo Toscano, Libro della Cocina* (An Anonymous Tuscan Cookbook) – gave a recipe for a show-stopping pastry case filled with live birds, to thrill guests at the table. Another from the same period can be found in the German cookbook *Registrum Coquine* (The Kitchen Register) and revealed the elite nature of the dish. 'To make a pastry for noblemen', it instructed, 'Take thrushes, starlings and blackbirds, or other kinds of birds [...] make a pastry and put it into a pan [...] And make a funnel. And mix eggs, saffron and rosewater and pour them in through the funnel. And this will be for Englishmen.' Blackbird pie funnels are still used to this day, a remarkable reminder of this ancient custom.

In terms of superstitions, blackbirds are unusually absent from British folk tales, but do have a starring role in Italian weather lore. According to tradition, the 29, 30 and 31 January are *I giorni della merla* or the 'Days of the Blackbird'. The story goes that the blackbird was originally white. At the end of one particularly harsh, snowy January, the bird was looking for shelter for herself and her chicks and found a warm chimney stack. The family of blackbirds took refuge inside the chimney for three long days and, when they emerged, had become permanently stained with soot. The weather lore also maintains that if *I giorni della merla* are particularly cold, spring will be early. But if the last three days of January are unusually mild, spring will be late and wet. The blackbird's beautiful voice, however, is always a welcome sign – *Quando canta il merlo, siamo fuori dell'inverno* ('When the blackbirds sings, winter has passed').

Lovebird

There was in their tiny tune
A dying fetch like broken words,
When I looked up at my love-birds
That Sunday afternoon.

THOMAS HARDY (1917)

Many species of bird form intense, long-lasting relationships, but lovebirds seem particularly smitten with each other. These petit, short-tailed birds, native to mainland Africa and Madagascar, mate for life and spend hours perched closely side by side. Much of their behaviour also resembles human courtship: lovebirds endlessly 'kiss' beaks, groom and snuggle up to each other. When one partner dies, the other lovebird is left bereft and in French, Italian and Spanish, lovebirds are called *inseparables*. Even the scientific name for the lovebird genus is *Agapornis*, a contraction of the ancient Greek for 'love', *agape*, and 'bird', *ornis*.

Most Westerners would, historically, have never seen a lovebird in the wild. But the Victorians successfully bred lovebirds as caged pets, either keeping devoted pairs or a solitary lovebird, the latter creating a strong bond with its keeper. This ardent loyalty appealed to the sentimental Victorian, who also took the bird as a metaphor for romantic, dedicated love. William Makepeace Thackeray, in his 1860 novel *Lovel the Widower*, followed the life of a newly bereaved husband and his struggles. He wrote of the pining of a 'love-bird without his mate', a trope repeated throughout nineteenth-century literature. Lovebirds also represented longed-for intimacy, an idea often employed in poetry. Many a tightly corseted verse, such as Joseph Ashby-Sterry's *My Lady's Boudoir*, feverishly drew on the imagery:

> She can tell to her love-birds her sorrow,
> When no interloper is nigh;
> She may hope for the joy of tomorrow,
> Or hopelessly have 'a good cry'!

Caged birds, especially those as devoted to each other as lovebirds, also captured the attention of artists and writers keen to express something of the confinement of conjugal relationships. Marriage was, for them, a gilded cage, but a cage nevertheless. As American author Ernest de Lancey Pierson wrote in his 1891 short story *A Bargain in Souls*, 'this house was no longer a love-birds nest, such as poets love to sing about, but a gilded cage whose inmates are struggling to be free.' In an 1896 magazine article, feminist writer Anna Bell called marriage a 'love-birds' cage' and couldn't imagine why 'any nice-minded person, anybody with the slightest delicacy of feeling' would opt for 'deliberate matrimony'.

While lovebirds are a relatively recent addition to the Western aviary, the idea of inseparable birds goes way back in time. Ancient Chinese literature also used mythical 'lovebirds' as a shorthand for romantic love; Bai Juyi, a poet of the Tang Dynasty, penned 'On high, we'd be two lovebirds flying wing to wing'. Early medieval Chinese legend spoke of birds that had only one eye and one wing. Male and female birds had to pair up and fly side by side to function effectively, a rather lovely allusion to married love.

Swan

*But at the last, when the swan is dying, it is said to sing
exceedingly sweetly as it dies. Likewise, when the proud
man departs this life, he delights still in the sweetness of this
world, and dying, he remembers the things which he did wrong.*

HUGH OF FOUILLOY (12TH CENTURY)

The swan is one of our most poignant birds. The idea of a 'swan-song' comes
from an age-old notion that the bird, just before it dies, sings a beautiful refrain,
a final arresting performance. For a phrase we still use today, it is startlingly
ancient. *Aesop's Fables*, written around the sixth century BCE, include the tale of
The Swan and his Owner, a story of a foolish man who buys a swan hoping it will
sing for his dinner guests. When the swan fails to make a sound, the enraged
man orders the swan to be killed and served up for supper, whereupon the bird
bursts into song knowing it is going to die. Subsequent authors, from Roman
naturalists to medieval philosophers, continued to peddle the idea. Over 2,000
years later, in 1612, English composer Orlando Gibbons published *The Silver Swan*,
a work that reiterated the idea of the bird's last lament:

> *The silver Swan, who, living, had no Note,*
> *when Death approached, unlocked her silent throat.*
> *Leaning her breast against the reedy shore,*
> *thus sang her first and last, and sang no more...*

People were enthralled by the swan's milky-white plumage. Chaucer dubbed it the 'snow-whyt swan' and many thought it was unlucky to kill such a heavenly, flawless bird. In Norse mythology, the sacred Well of Urd contained holy water that turned everything it touched white, including the world's first pair of swans and all their descendants. Celtic legend also talks of the swan as a bird with supernatural powers; in a number of Irish literary sources, swans are often female shapeshifters or humans disguised by a curse. In one of Ireland's best-known legends, *The Children of Lir*, a lord's four offspring are transformed into swans by their jealous stepmother and must stay that way for 900 years.

In northern European mythology, the idea of a swan-maiden also appears in various iterations. In many versions, a young man steals a magical garment from a swan-maiden he has fallen in love with. Without her enchanted piece of clothing, the swan-maiden cannot fly away and so must stay grounded with her new 'husband'. When the swan-maiden finally rediscovers her stolen apparel, she escapes and flies away, no doubt a metaphor for the dangers of forced love. Tchaikovsky's ballet *Swan Lake* is thought to have been inspired by one German swan-maiden folktale called *The Stolen Veil*. In it, a young man discovers a flock of enchanted swans who become maidens every night when they remove their head coverings. The young man steals the veil of the most beautiful maiden, preventing her turning back into a swam, and forces her to be his bride.

Mockingbird

Winged mimic of the woods! Thou motley fool!
Who shall thy gay buffoonery describe?
Thine every ready notes of ridicule
Pursue thy fellows still with jest and gibe.

RICHARD HENRY WILDE: *TO THE MOCKING-BIRD* (19TH CENTURY)

The mockingbird belongs to the Americas. From the Canadian border to
South America, this versatile vocalist is famed for its remarkable repertoire.
The taxonomic name for the northern mockingbird, one of the best known
of the family, is *Mimus polyglottos*, the 'many-tongued mimic', a name that
perfectly captures this remarkable creature's ear for impersonation. While some
mockingbirds have at least 50 songs in their vocal catalogue, some have 100 or
more. Each performance can include a wide range of samples from other birds'
calls, insect and frog noises, and – in urban areas – even human-made sounds
such as car alarms or mechanical noises.

American settlers and European visitors alike were impressed by the
mockingbird's remarkable choral abilities. Renowned German birder Karl Russ,
in the late nineteenth century, declared the northern mockingbird 'the most
excellent of all songsters among birds', praising its melodies to the heavens.
'They are not the soft sounds of the flute or of the hautboy [oboe] that I hear,
but the sweeter notes of Nature's own music. The mellowness of the song,
the varied modulations and graduations, the extent of its compass, the great
brilliancy of execution, are unrivalled. There is probably no bird in the world
that possesses all the musical qualifications of this "king of song".

For many indigenous peoples of America, however, the mockingbird was already one of their most celebrated birds and central to their origin stories. The Hopi of Arizona, for example, said the mockingbird gave the world its different ethnicities and languages. For the Bribri of Costa Rica, mockingbirds were protected from harm as they were said to have served as helpers when their god, Sibö, created the world. And for the Pueblo of the southwestern United States, the mockingbird was considered wise in the ways of song and language, and responsible for granting humans the power of speech. Many Native American cultures also named the bird after its tendency to imitate other avians: the Chicasaw people called it *foshi' taloowa'* (bird singer) while the Choctaw called the mockingbird the *hushi balbaha* (bird that speaks a foreign language). In English, the earliest appearance of the word 'mockingbird' is often said to come from the 1676 Royal Society of London *Philosophical Transactions*, but an earlier text pre-empts this description. In his early seventeenth-century work, *The Description of Mary-Land*, cartographer John Speed warmly described America's 'Mock-bird' and 'its imitation of all other Singing-birds', creating one of the earliest English descriptions of the American continent's most extraordinary birds.

Bittern

...of all those sounds, there is none so dismally hollow as the booming of the bittern. It is impossible for words to give those who have not heard this evening-call an adequate idea of its solemnity.

OLIVER GOLDSMITH (1774)

The bittern is the *basso profundo* of the choir. Its sonorous, booming voice, sent from the reed beds, can travel for kilometres and has, over the centuries, been interpreted as the cries of eerie monsters. The elusive Australasian bittern is also known as the 'bunyip bird', its mating call mistaken for a terrifying creature thought to lurk on the banks of swamps and rivers in southeastern Australia. In Slavic mythology, the Drekavac is a tormented, night-roaming creature who takes the souls of the sinful. In one version of the legend, when the Drekavac is heard near a pond and scares away the fisherman, a courageous boy captures the beast, which turns out to be a bittern. On the west coast of Scotland, tales of the boobrie – a mythical, shapeshifting bird that preys on livestock – were thought to have been inspired by the bittern and its low, cattle-like sigh.

In Sherlock Holmes' most famous adventure *The Hound of the Baskervilles*, published in 1902, the uncanny moan heard across the moors is initially suggested to belong to a bittern. No one was quite sure, however, how the bittern made its unusually low, thunderous groan. Medieval scribes believed the bittern put its beak beneath the water or blew down a reed to magnify its voice. In Oliver Goldsmith's ambitious 1774 work, *A History of the Earth, and Animated Nature*, he noted: 'The common people are of opinion, that it thrusts its bill into a reed that serves as a pipe for swelling the note above its natural pitch; while others [...] imagine that the bittern puts its head under water, and then violently blowing produces its boomings.'

The Anglo-Saxons, who so often named birds after their sounds rather than their looks, called the bittern the *hæferblæte*, 'goat bleater', or the *rāredumle*, 'reed boomer'. By the Middle Ages, the bittern was awash with folk names, most of which drew on its rumbling, thrumming call. From 'mire-drum' to 'bitter bump', most vernacular names celebrated the bird's booms. Walter Scott wrote of 'the deep cry of the bog-blitter, or bull-of-the-bog', while Chaucer enjoyed the expression 'As a bitore bombleth in the myre'.

In Maori culture, the bittern, or *matuku*, was thought to cry from loneliness and is known as the 'grief bird'. In an ancient lament, the bereaved singer compares themselves to the sorrowful bird:

> *I am an angry spirit,*
> *A hawk screaming in winter*
> *A bittern hooting in the swamp.*

Kingfisher

Alcyone compress'd
Seven days sits brooding on her watery nest
A wintry queen; her sire at length in kind,
Calms every storm, and hushes every wind.

JOHN DRYDEN (17TH CENTURY)

In Greek mythology Ceyx and Alcyone were husband and wife and, unusually for classical legends, very happily married. Their relationship, however, angered Zeus, the god of sky and thunder, who killed Ceyx while at sea. When Alcyone learned of her beloved's death, she threw herself into the waves, upon which the gods took mercy on the couple and turned both into kingfishers. When Alcyone, now a beautiful bird, tried to make a nest on the beach, the waves threatened to destroy it. Alycone's father Aeolus, who was also the god of storms, intervened and calmed the winds for a few brief days, allowing Alycone's eggs to hatch. This handful of days around the winter solstice, when the seas were calm and the weather clement, became known as 'Alcyone-days' or 'Halcyon-days', a phrase we still use to describe a time when things were unusually happy or calm. Amulets made from kingfisher body parts have also been worn since classical times. Timotheos of Gaza, a fifth-century CE author, described a gold charm containing the heart of a kingfisher, which would protect the wearer from thunder or lightning.

The common kingfisher, which is more at home on riverbanks than stormy seas, has attracted plenty of interest over the years. Its iridescent blue-and-orange plumage, and razor-quick plunges into the water, have earned it some gorgeous epithets. The Italians called it the *piombino* or plummet. Its sublime hunting ability was recognized by many cultures – the French call it *martin-pêcheur*, the Spanish *martín pescador*, both of which translate to the 'fisherman martin'. In English, the bird has been recognized as the 'king-fisher', monarch of the river, since the fifteenth century. For Germanic and Scandinavian speakers, however, the bird is named after its glacier-blue feathers – the 'ice-bird'.

The kingfisher was also significant in ancient China. Kingfisher feather crowns or headdresses, known as *feng guan*, were typically worn by empresses or brides on their wedding day. In many parts of China, however, kingfisher plumage was difficult to obtain and had to be imported, at vast expense, from places such as Cambodia and Thailand. Wearing kingfisher feathers not only displayed wealth and prestige but there was also other symbolism at work. In early Chinese poetry, kingfishers were seen as charming, virtuous birds. Cai Yong, a second-century CE scholar and calligrapher, wrote about kingfishers 'bringing cyan tints to life' but being constantly hunted by fowlers. Only in the courtyard of a high-status man, he maintained, would the kingfisher be safe: 'With docile hearts entrusted to the purity of mi'lord; Cock and hen are here ensured their hundred'. The symbolism of the kingfisher, therefore, was deeply wedded to ideas about imperial femininity – a gentle, fine-looking maiden was only safe if carefully guarded by a righteous gentleman.

Ibis

It is at once a splendid and rather forbidding creature, with bald black head and snaky neck, black feet and legs boldly patterned with hexagonal scales...

ELIZABETH RIEFSTAHL (1949)

In ancient Egypt, pharaohs were often mummified. But this intriguing practice of preserving flesh for the afterlife wasn't just reserved for humans. From baby crocodiles to domesticated dogs, many millions of animals were wrapped up for eternity. And, when it came to Egyptian birds, perhaps none was quite so favoured as the ibis.

The sacred African ibis, and to a lesser extent, two other species of ibis, played a central role in ancient Egyptian religion. More than four million mummified ibises were found in the catacombs of Tuna-el-Gebel, about 250 kilometres (150 miles) south of Cairo. Another 1.75 million were also unearthed from an ancient burial ground at Saqqara.

Animals were sacrificed to propitiate the gods and ask for their favour. Ibises were the bird of Thoth, the god of wisdom, magic and writing, who was often represented as an ibis or an ibis-headed man. Thoth was also a divine arbitrator and helped judge the souls of the dead. Those who feared they might not pass muster at their divine reckoning were encouraged, while still alive, to make an offering to Thoth. Other people sacrificed an ibis hoping for a long life, success in romance or a speedy recovery from illness.

But why were ibises the birds of choice? In ancient Egypt, the sacred ibis would have been a common bird. In practical terms, ibises were fabulous pest controllers, eating the snails and insects that infested ponds and swamplands. There were also fearless in the face of snakes, a quality that didn't go unnoticed by later Greek and Latin writers. Geographer and author Gaius Julius Solinus, writing in the third century CE, noted that:

'The swamps of Arabia send forth swarms of winged serpents, whose venom is so quick-acting, that, after a bite, death follows more quickly than pain. The ibis, from an innate wisdom, go out aroused and in readiness for battle and devastates this foreign evil before it reaches the borders of their land [...] For which reason, ibis are deservedly held to be holy, and no-one may injure them.'

Quite what the 'winged serpent' was isn't certain, but the ibis was clearly in early scholars' good books. The ibis was also sacred to the moon. Some believed the association came from the bird's crescent like-beak, others wrote that the ibis hatched its eggs 'in the same number of days that the goddess takes to wax and wane' – in other words, a full lunar month. Only Isidore of Seville, in the seventh century CE, had anything strange to add about the ibis: it 'purges itself by spurting water into its anus with its beak', he scribbled with fevered imagination, an idea that was as unintentionally hilarious as it was wrong.

Plover

But when the cry of the plover is abroad we know [...]
that Winter is old and broken and shuffling north.

FIONA MACLEOD (1906)

Plovers are part of a larger family that include lapwings and dotterels. A wonderfully cosmopolitan group of waders, plovers are found across the world, apart from in polar extremes and scorching deserts. Characterized by short bills that pick among the pebbles and quick bursts of running, these endearing birds have long been subject to legend and folklore. Many species are migratory and their homecoming heralded the beginning of spring. An old Scottish rhyme explained that warmer weather was on its way when the whistling cries of the curlew (see page 62) or plover rang out across the shoreline:

> *Whaup, Whimbrel an' Plover*
> *Whan these whustle the worst o't 's over.*

In Iceland, too, the arrival of the plover signalled an end to winter. The first sighting of the *lóa*, or golden plover, is still recognized as the return of spring, an event that has earned the bird the nickname *vorboðinn ljúfi* (sweet spring herald). Nineteenth-century Icelandic poet Páll Ólafsson's ode to the plover celebrated the landscape's reawakening:

> *The golden plover has arrived to banish the snow*
> *To banish the boredom, that it can do.*
> *It has told me the whimbrel will arrive soon,*
> *sunshine in the valley and blooms in the meadow.*

Not every story, however, fêted the plover. Russian folklore explained how the plover got its wailing cry. When God created the Earth, he wanted to include seas, river and lakes, so he asked all the birds to bring water to their appointed places. The plover, however, refused and was punished by never being allowed to approach a sea or stream to quench its thirst. Instead, it would only be allowed to drink from the meagre pools left behind between stones and pebbles. The plover's wailful cry is, therefore, from its continuous, unslaked thirst.

Others thought the plover's cry uncanny. Robert Burns' *The Brigs of Ayr* (1786) spoke of 'The deep-ton'd plovers grey, wild-whistling o'er the hill' and the wader, along with the curlew, was classed as one of the Seven Whistlers (see page 64) or part of a spectral group of birds and hounds called Gabriel Ratchets. These strange, yelping creatures would show themselves to someone who had a loved one close to death or represent the ghosts of unbaptized babies. In Gaelic, the plover was the *feadag*, a word also given to the flute or whistle and was thought to survive, not on food or water, but only on wind. The *feadag* was also the name given to the first week of March; a week of whistling, eerie gusts.

Hummingbird

What can there be in common between this graceful little creature and the monstrous idol of the Aztecs?

ALBERT RÉVILLE (1884)

For such a tiny bird, the hummingbird punches well above its weight when it comes to mythology. Native to the Americas, it was often seen as an intermediary, with the ability to flit between human and sacred worlds. In ancient Mesoamerica, only three birds were thought to have the capacity to fly between Earth and the heavens: the eagle (see page 140), the vulture (see page 91) and the hummingbird. Of these, the hummingbird worked on behalf of the gods, sending messages to guide and warn people.

The hummingbird was one of the most significant birds for the Aztecs and represented Huitzilopochtli, the god of sun and warfare. Huitzilopochtli is often translated as 'hummingbird of the south' and, as the solar deity, was said to be in constant struggle with the forces of darkness. This exhausting, never-ending skirmish could only be sustained by ritually 'feeding' Huitzilopochtli with blood, either in the form of sacrifice or daily self-bloodletting. Far from being a macabre, pointless exercise, this ancient practice was based on a worldview that saw people owing a huge debt of gratitude to the gods and that hard work and pain were appropriate ways to give thanks. It's interesting that both dead warriors and women who died in childbirth, people who experienced agony for others, were said to turn into sacred hummingbirds.

The hummingbird was also linked to pre-Columbian ideas about heroism on the battlefield. The bird's long, sharp beak resembled a sword or a piercing tool such as a cactus thorn, the latter used by warriors and rulers to draw blood from themselves. Hummingbirds were admired not just for their beauty, but for their ferocity in the face of predators or larger birds. This, combined with their speed and aerial adroitness (hummingbirds are the only birds able to fly backwards), easily endeared them to early cultures who valued bravery and physical skill.

The hummingbird also represented the souls of the dead. This hovering, darting sprite of a bird was sometimes viewed as a reincarnation of a dead child, flitting among the living, or the soul of a deceased loved one who had come back to comfort their relatives. Several species of hummingbird also go into a prolonged, seasonal sleep called torpor, which was interpreted as a kind of death. Hummingbirds, symbolically, loitered precariously between life and death; the Aztecs, for example, believed that hummingbirds were resurrected by the arrival of the rainy season and, as such, belonged to both worlds. Such a divine being, therefore, was never hunted or persecuted.

One of the most famous hummingbirds is among the Nazca Line creatures, geoglyphs made by indigenous Peruvian people sometime between 400 BCE and 500 CE. This giant representation, at nearly 100 metres (330 feet) long, may have been created to ensure the return of the rainy season, when the hummingbird magically 'came back to life'.

Vulture

The Vulture is the dead body's enemy [...] it swoops upon it as though it were an adversary and devours it, and watches a man who is in the throes of death.

CLAUDIUS AELIANUS (2ND–3RD CENTURY CE)

The vulture, a bird that plays a crucial role in nature's food chain, has sometimes struggled with its reputation. For some cultures, an animal that survives by eating dead carrion, or 'stealing' another creature's kill, was to be feared or maligned. For others, however, the vulture played a key role in belief systems about the sacred and the feminine.

Ancient Greek authors, writing about earlier Egyptian culture, noted that all vultures were thought to be females. In Egyptian hieroglyphics, the vulture was drawn to denote the word 'mother' and often used in conjunction with other symbols. The hieroglyph of a vulture with a flail, for instance, was used to represent the name Mut, the mother goddess of Thebes. Royal wives, priestesses and female pharaohs also wore bird crowns in the form of a vulture draped across the top of the head. These ornate headdresses were thought to embody Nekhbet, the vulture goddess. Nekhbet was typically depicted as a vulture or as a woman with the head of a vulture, and was the deity of motherhood, protection and sovereignty. The vulture, in Egyptian mythology, was a bird revered for its protective nature and ability to soar high to the heavens. Many images of Nekhbet show her hovering, wings shielding the royal image, and clutching a shen ring, a symbol of eternal protection.

Not all descriptions of the vulture, however, were so flattering. Three thousand years ago King Solomon, according to legend, punished a committee of vultures for not protecting him from the scorching sun. Henceforth, he cursed that all vultures 'shall forever feel the heat of the sun, the bite of the wind and the beating of the rain on their bare necks.'

Both the Greeks and the Romans thought the vulture a bird that took pleasure in feasting on the bodies of the dead. In Homer's *Iliad*, for example, warriors lying dead on the arena were 'far dearer to the vultures than to their wives'. Superstition held that the bird could even predict where a battle might take place, by following lines of marching troops. Writing in the third century CE, scholar and author Claudius Aelianus maintained that 'Vultures even follow in the wake of armies in foreign parts, knowing by prophetic instinct that they are going to war and that every battle provides corpses.'

In the Americas, the vulture was also associated with mortality but revered for its transformative power to change death and decay into new life. By eating carrion, and the bodies of the fallen or sacrificed, vultures were thought able to release the spirit and carry a soul to heaven on its wings. The vulture's habit of nesting in dark cavities and caves – liminal openings to the underworld – also gave it sacred power.

FEATHERS

For as long as humans have been among birds, we have envied their ability to fly. We have jealously watched their ability to reel, swoop and soar. We have longed for the freedom of the skies, for a connection to the distant and mysterious heavens. And perhaps no object best represents that yearning than the feather. Throughout history and prehistory, and across continents, many cultures have endowed feathers with magical or superstitious power. From ritual clothing and costume to headdresses and crowns, feathers have long been incorporated into ceremonial dress in the hope that its wearer could absorb some of the attributes of birds. Other ritual objects – such as drums or rattles – were also decorated with feathers to symbolize the sky spirits, or assist communication between the human and spiritual realms.

Different feathers could hold different meanings and, equally importantly, convey status. A feather from a bird that was difficult to hunt or capture, or a particularly beautiful, rare feather, was often reserved for the highest ranking or most respected members of a community. Ostrich (see page 27) feathers, for example, dazzled and impressed almost universally. In ancient Egypt, Tutankhamen was interred with a fan made from feathers that had come from an ostrich killed by the pharaoh himself. In medieval England, crusading knights adorned their helmets with exotic ostrich feathers as a sign of bravery and nobility. And in Regency England, far from the horrors of the battlefield, high-society women adorned their heads with plumes of ostrich feathers, a highly conspicuous display of wealth and exclusive good taste.

Cardinal

The bird call'd the Cardinal, is about the bigness of a Wood-lark; of a scarlet colour; and has a beautiful tuft of feathers on its head, and sings sweetly. For these, the Spanish give ten or twelve crowns a bird, to send to Spain.

THOMAS SALMON (1739)

Thomas Salmon, the English historian, was a well-travelled man. In his fiftieth year, no spring chicken, he embarked on a round-the-world trip with Commodore George Anson and saw all manner of new and astounding creatures on the way. In Mexico, novel animals hid in every corner. From flying squirrels to sloths, armadillos to wasp-sized hummingbirds (see page 88), Salmon was both surprised and delighted by what he encountered. Other European voyagers also coveted the New World's bounty and Salmon noted that Spanish traders would pay handsomely for one particular bird – the cardinal. Prices were exorbitant for this little red avian, a native to the eastern American states and south into Mexico, and huge sums of money exchanged hands. In the 1730s, just one captured cardinal netted a month's wages for a skilled labourer.

It seems everyone wanted the cardinal as an exotic prize. Pierre-François-Xavier de Charlevoix, a French priest, wrote one of the earliest descriptive accounts of North America. While Spanish sailors were paying top prices for cardinals in Mexico, it seems similar deals were being struck further north. 'There are some at Paris', he wrote, 'that were transported from Louisiana, and I believe they will make their Fortune in France, if they can breed them there like Canary-Birds. The Sweetness of Its Song, the Brilliancy of its Plumage, which is of a fine Scarlet, a little Tuft of Feathers they have upon their Head, and which pretty well resembles the Crowns which Painters give to *Indian* Kings and *Americans*, seems to confirm to them, the Empire of the Air.'

The cardinal was named for its resemblance to the red garments worn by Roman Catholic senior officials. As noted in Francis Willughby's ornithological observations in 1678, 'by the Portuguese it is commonly called the Cardinal bird, because of its scarlet colour and seems to wear on its Head a red hat', but the English initially called it by a different name. 'It is brought into England out of Virginia', explained Willughby, 'whence, from its rare singing, it is called the *Virginian Nightingale*.'

For some indigenous Americans, the cardinal was more than an expensive trophy. The Cherokee saw the cardinal, or 'red bird', as sacred, a carrier of important news. It was also said to have got its scarlet colour from a good deed. A wolf, who had been blinded with mud by a racoon, asked the cardinal to peck off the baked dirt from his eyes. When the cardinal fulfilled its promise, the wolf showed the bird a rock full of bright pigment. The cardinal, thrilled with the colour, painted its entire body and was, from that moment on, the 'red bird'.

Peacock

But spoke again: 'If true art thou,
Take thou the Peacock's sacred vow.'
Her listening maidens caught the word,
And forth they brought the royal bird...

LETITIA ELIZABETH LANDON (1835)

Native to the Indian subcontinent, common peafowl were introduced into Greece around the fifth century BCE. For all their embellished appeal, both peacocks and peahens were initially farmed as game-fowl, an enterprise that earned handsome rewards for those who were good at it. Varro, a Roman writer and a farmer in his own right, described peafowl breeders grossing '60,000 sesterces a year out of these birds'. A Roman legionary under Caesar, by contrast, earned just 900 sesterces.

The bird graced the tables of the wealthy and powerful. Like all displays of conspicuous consumption, however, peafowl-eating also drew its jeering critics. In *The Satyricon*, from the first century CE, Petronius ridiculed the pointless ostentatiousness of it all:

> *Insatiable luxury crumbles the walls of war;*
> *To satiate gluttony, peacocks in coops are brought*
> *Arrayed in gold plumage like Babylon tapestry rich.*
> *Numidian guinea-fowls, capons, all perish for thee...*

In its native lands, however, the peacock was revered. In Hindu culture the peacock, or *mayura* in Sanskrit, was a sacred bird and appeared in a number of legends. In the *Ramayana*, one of India's most epic and ancient poems, for example, a god called Indra sheltered under the wing of a peacock. As a gesture of thanks, Indra blessed the peacock with two gifts – a thousand 'eyes' and a fearlessness of snakes. The name *mayura* is thought to mean 'killer of serpents'.

Lord Krishna, one of Hinduism's most significant deities, is often depicted with a peacock feather in his crown. In Hindu mythology, Lord Krishna was reincarnated from his predecessor Lord Rama. One legend tells of Lord Rama and his consort, the goddess Sita, getting lost in a jungle and desperately needing water. A peacock appeared and promised to guide them to a crystal-clear spring. To help them follow the bird, the peacock dropped its vibrant tail feathers – one by one – until they reached safety. The peacock, now featherless, died but, in recognition of its courage, Rama vowed to honour the bird in his next incarnation. When Rama came back as Lord Krishna, true to his word, he wore a peacock feather on his head in tribute to the bird's great sacrifice.

In medieval England, the peacock was also considered a blessed bird. Since at least the fifth century, and the writing of Augustine, the peacock's flesh was said to be incorruptible – it would never decay – and the peacock's 'eyes' were thought to represent God's omniscience. The peafowl's fearlessness against snakes and supposed ability to eat toxic plants also encouraged people to believe in the bird's immortal nature. Pilgrim badges, souvenirs bought at religious places, often came in the form of peacocks, while medieval knights were said to swear a 'Vow of the Peacock' – rather like a new year's resolution – to recommit themselves to another year of chivalrous good deeds and derring-do.

Pelican

Look here and mark, her sickly birds to feed
How freely this kind Pelican doth bleed.

GEORGE WITHER (1622)

In medieval bestiaries, few animals were extolled quite as freely as the pelican. While many birds were falsely branded as agents of the devil, slothful or just plain stupid, the pelican was possibly the most saintly bird in Christendom. The reason for this religious approval came from a fundamental misunderstanding of how a pelican fed its young, an error that also probably saved the bird from centuries of persecution.

Writing in the seventh century CE, Isidore of Seville noted there were rumours that the pelican could perform an extraordinary miracle: 'It is reported, if it may be true', he wrote, 'that this bird kills its offspring, mourns them for three days, and finally wounds itself and revives its children by sprinkling them with its own blood.' Isidore, like many scholars working in the early medieval period, had mined Roman and Greek classical sources for all kinds of information about animals, birds and fantastical creatures. In the third or fourth century CE, a book called the *Physiologus* had already made the outrageous claim that the pelican killed its unruly young and then, full of remorse, revived them with its own blood. The *Physiologus* then went on to compare this strange but wondrous behaviour to the story of the salvation. Namely, that Christ's blood revived Man, even when he had sinned against God.

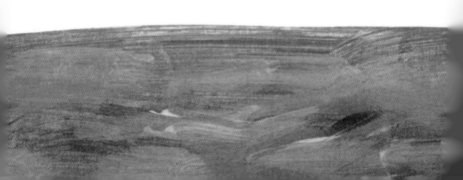

Scholars such as Isidore of Seville, and countless others, copied and translated the story of the pious pelican. The devout waterbird also became a common symbol in liturgical and secular art. One of the most famous depictions of Queen Elizabeth I, for example, is the 'Pelican Portrait' attributed to painter Nicholas Hilliard. Finished around 1575, it shows the sovereign wearing a brooch of a mother pelican, a jewel that represented Elizabeth's self-sacrifice to the nation. From stone carvings to painted crucifixes, the image of the pious pelican feeding its chicks from her pierced chest was routinely employed into the nineteenth century and beyond. In 1880, proponents of the Arts and Crafts movement were still evoking the legend, with artist and designer Edward Burne-Jones including one in the stained-glass windows he created for St Martin's in Brampton, Cumbria. Nearly 2,000 years after the pelican myth was first captured in the *Physiologus*, a small church near the Lake District was getting its very own pious pelican.

Song Thrush

At once a voice arose among
The bleak twigs overhead
In a full-hearted evensong
Of joy illimited...

THOMAS HARDY (1900)

The song thrush, with its buff brown feathers, often goes unnoticed. Until, that is, it starts to sing. The bird, for its body size, has one of the loudest and most eloquent calls, full of musicality and variation. With its ear for melody, the young song thrush will often copy its parents, and blend these notes with those from other birds to create a vast repertoire. Even its Latin name, *Turdus phiomelos*, celebrates the song thrush's remarkable voice. In Greek mythology, Philomena was subject to a terrible act of violence by her sister's husband. He raped her and cut out her tongue, an act of such horror that the gods turned her into a songbird. The name Philomena translates to *philo,* 'lover', and *melos,* 'song'.

There are some lovely, lyrical English folk-names for the song thrush, many of which have evolved from the Anglo-Saxon *thrysce*, including 'thrusher' in Berkshire, 'dirsh' in Somerset, 'throstle' in Yorkshire and 'thirstle' in Devon. Over the centuries, many a writer has tried to capture the song thrush's melodies in words. Shakespeare's *Winter's Tale* tried a simple version – 'With heigh! with heigh! the thrush and the jay' – while Victorian twitcher William MacGillivray gave his poetic rendition of the bird's 'wild melodies':

Sing to the lov'd ones whose nest is near.
Qui, qui, qui, kweeu, quip,
Tiurru, tiurru, chipiwi.
Too-tee, too-tee, chiu choo,
Chirri, chirri, chooee,
Quiu, qui, qui.

The song thrush's sweet voice was often compared to other, less tuneful birds. Tudor poet John Skelton, in *The Book of Phillip Sparrow*, described 'The throstle with her warbling; The starling with her brabling' ('brabling' is an old word for squabbling).

Some strange beliefs also attached themselves to the song thrush. Writing in the seventeenth century, the great naturalist Johannes Jonstonus claimed that all song thrushes were deaf. It was also thought that if you captured a young song thrush, its wild parents would try to poison the offspring through the bars of the cage by dropping belladonna seeds into its mouth. Perhaps the most outlandish claim was that song thrushes grew new legs every seven or ten years. Writing to *Hardwicke's Science Gossip*, in 1867, people reported having witnessed birds casting off their old legs and acquiring a fresh pair:

'A thrush kept in a cage at Lyneside (Kirklinton), said to be about ten years of age, has recently acquired a new pair of legs, the old ones drying up and dropping off. The first time I saw the bird, the new feet were protruding from the front of the knee joint, and looked soft and light-coloured. On my second visit they had lengthened considerably, but were not of any use to the bird. Afterwards I saw it when the new feet were used, and the old on shrivelling up, soon after which the old feet dropped off.'

Bluebird

Truly in the East
The white bean
And the great corn-plant
Are tied with the white lightning.
Listen! rain approaches!
The voice of the bluebird is heard.

TRADITIONAL NAVAJO SONG

There are three exquisite but different species of birds that are all called 'bluebirds' in North America. The Eastern bluebird, the Western bluebird and the Mountain bluebird do, however, share one obvious similarity – they all have strikingly sapphire plumage.

The Pima, a Native American group who traditionally lived in Arizona, have a legend about how the bluebird and coyote got their characteristic colours. The beautiful bluebird was once a creature with dull, dreary feathers. He bathed in a magical lake for four days in a row, warbling a special song, and on the fourth day his plumage finally turned a beautiful, bright blue. A coyote, who had green fur, had watched the bluebird and also wanted to change colour. He copied the bluebird's actions and, on day four, also turned a dazzling cerulean. The coyote was so pleased with his new sky-blue fur that, self-admiring, he didn't watch where he was running. He crashed into a stump and fell into the dust, turning his blue fur into the dull, dusty brown that he still wears today.

The bluebird was also a harbinger of spring and celebrated by a number of indigenous groups. In Iroquois mythology, the bluebird's soft, winsome song was said to drive away Tawiscaron, a malevolent deity of winter, death and night. For other cultures, such as the Navajo, the bluebird was closely associated with the east, the rising sun, and the return of the dawn; the bird was also an important symbol of fertility and part of a girl's puberty rite. One ceremony, *Kinaaldá*, was a four-day event that celebrated a girl's transition to womanhood.

Traditionally, a special medicine was prepared that the initiate had to carry for the duration, and included salt, skins of bluebirds and medicinal plants that had been placed inside a bluebird's nest and retrieved after the birds had sat on them.

For colonial US settlers, the bluebird also became an adopted symbol of dawn and springtime. In 1896, one of America's best-loved poets, Emily Dickinson, penned a tribute to this much-admired bird:

> *Before you thought of spring,*
> *Except as a surmise,*
> *You see, God bless his suddenness,*
> *A fellow in the skies*
> *Of independent hues,*
> *A little weather-worn,*
> *Inspiriting habiliments*
> *Of indigo and brown.*

By the twentieth century, bluebirds were such an established emblem of hope and happiness they featured in many a popular song. From *Bluebird of Happiness* to *Bluebirds in the Moonlight*, Stateside songwriters delved into the bird's symbolism. Perhaps the best-known song of all was *(There'll Be Bluebirds Over) The White Cliffs of Dover*. This rousing Second World War anthem was designed to stir hope and optimism in the darkest months of 1941. It did the trick and became wildly popular, despite England never having had a bluebird anywhere near its shores.

Sparrow

In the vicinity of London [..], pots of unglazed delf ware of a sub-oval shape, with a narrow hole for an entrance, are fixed upon the walls of houses, several feet below the eave, and the Sparrows finding a domicile so suited to their habits, very soon take possession of every pot.

GEORGE MONTAGU (1833)

In the middle of the eighteenth century, a child was hanged for an extraordinary crime. Writing about it only a few years after, agricultural author William Ellis recounted the true story of 'How a Boy used to rob Houses by means of a tame Sparrow'.

'I have read of an arch Thief, that was very young in Years, but an old Practitioner in the horrid Wickedness of Thievery; for, it is recorded, he had stole at times to the Value of five hundred Pounds. His Name was Rawdry Audry, who, under sixteen Years of Age, after having been several times in Newgate, tried and convicted for several Crimes, and, after a little suffering for them, discharged, was at last condemned to die for a Robbery, and hang'd at Tyburn.'

Audry would get a young sparrow and train it to fly from his hand. Once he had tamed the bird, Audry would wander the wealthy areas of London looking for open sash windows. When he saw one, Audry would encourage his sparrow to fly into the house and then knock on the door innocently asking to retrieve his pet. Once inside, the boy would grab not only his bird but any items of value and flit back into the streets. It's a remarkable story but, in many ways, represents the odd relationship people had with the humble house sparrow. For many folk, the sparrow was a familiar creature and one that could be put to use. While Audry's case was probably unique, from medieval times to the nineteenth century, both city dwellers and country folk deliberately fixed clay bottles to house walls to encourage sparrows to nest. Once filled, the sparrows could be caught and eaten. The same practice was also reported in France, the Netherlands and colonial America. Many an early cookbook features recipes for sparrows, including 'sparrow pie, sparrow pudding, and roast sparrows, spitted closely on long sticks or skewers'.

From Bangladesh to Morocco, Greece to England, it was thought that eating sparrows acted as an aphrodisiac, as the birds are such prodigious breeders. The *Kama Sutra* recommended sparrows' eggs and sparrow meat for prolonged love making, while medieval German physician Albertus Magnus also prescribed sparrow flesh to 'enkindle sexual desire'. Seventeenth-century English physician Nicholas Culpeper subscribed to the belief that 'The brain of Sparrows being eaten provoke lust exceedingly', but too much of a good thing, however, could be fatal. Sparrows were thought to live short lives because they were so carnal: 'His blood, and spirit, and pith, and marrow spends', wrote poet John Donne in 1633, 'Ill steward of himself, himself in three years ends'.

Wren

The wren, the wren, the king of all birds,
St. Stephen's Day was caught in the furze...

TRADITIONAL IRISH FOLK SONG (19TH CENTURY)

In many ancient cultures, animals were bound up in divine rituals. Across time and societies, certain special creatures were the focus of processions, often taken from house to house, before being sacrificed or set free. Victorian anthropologist James George Frazer collected a number of these rites in his seminal work *The Golden Bough*. From the bear parade of the Gilyak, in northern Asia, to the snake ceremonies of the Mirasans of Punjab, Frazer believed these highly ritualized 'performances' plugged into practices that were thousands of years old. The best known of all of these, he maintained, was the 'hunting of the wren' – a custom practised across Europe but especially in Ireland, southern France and the Isle of Man.

In Ireland, Wren Day took place on St Stephen's Day, 26 December. The men and boys from a particular village would hunt for a wren, kill it, and attach it to the top of a pole decorated with seasonal foliage and ribbons. The wren hunters, who were often dressed in greenery or garish clothing, would then parade the pole around the parish, chanting songs in return for food or money. In the Manx version of 'hunting the wren', the bird would also be given a mock funeral and buried in the local churchyard. Frazer recorded a similar custom in the south of France. On the first Sunday of December, youngsters in Carcassonne would go out beating the bushes, looking for a wren. The first to kill one was proclaimed the 'king' and the wren carried back into town, aloft on a pole. In Spain the *cacería del rey Charlo* (hunt of King Charles) involved a similar expedition and wren-pole procession.

Understanding the events of 'wren day' involves digging deeper into the bird's age-old symbolism. Many European cultures have long-called the wren the 'little king' or 'hedge king' and believed anyone who killed the bird would suffer misfortune. In England, for example, the robin and wren were viewed as sacred husband and wife and it was extremely unlucky to harm either – hence the saying 'The robin and the wren are God's cock and hen'. In France, anyone who destroyed a wren would be cursed with painful hands or feet, while in Scotland, the wren was the 'Lady of Heaven's Hen', and anyone who assaulted the bird would receive 'malisons' or curses:

> *Malisons, malisons, mair than ten,*
> *That harry the Ladye of Heaven's hen!*

So why hurt a bird that, for the rest of the year, was so revered? Frazer had a theory. 'The worshipful animal is killed with special solemnity once a year', he wrote, 'and before or immediately after death he is promenaded from door to door, that each of his worshippers may receive a portion of the divine virtues that are supposed to emanate from the dead or dying god.'

Cormorant

Thence up he flew, and on the tree of life,
The middle tree and highest there that grew,
Sat like a cormorant; yet not true life
Thereby regain'd, but sat devising death...

JOHN MILTON (1667)

In the middle of the seventeenth century, the English poet John Milton did the cormorant a great disservice. In his epic poem *Paradise Lost*, Milton described the Devil breaking into the Garden of Eden and perching high up in The Tree of Life, 'like a cormorant'. Quite why he chose this agile, sleek diving bird as an emblem of Satan isn't clear. He may have been delving into classical literature, inspired by Homer's *Iliad*, where the gods Athena and Apollo, disguised as vultures, crouch in Zeus's oak tree to watch a duel unfold.

More likely, however, is that Milton was simply repeating common tropes about this much-maligned bird, a creature that seemed to represent self-indulgence, gluttony and evil-doings. Writing in the sixteenth century, English clergyman Robert Cawdrey used the cormorant as an allegory for human avarice: 'As the glutton who overchargeth his stomach with meat is compelled to spew and cast it up again: so the greed, covetous cormorant, that gathereth great riches and devoureth and swalloweth great substance, shall lost is again: for God shall even draw it out of his belly.'

Shakespeare knew the symbolism too and employed it in his plays. In *Richard II*, for example, John of Gaunt – knowing that he is about die – speaks truth to the deficient Richard about his recklessness and greed:

> *His rash fierce blaze of riot cannot last,*
> *For violent fires soon burn out themselves;*
> *Small showers last long, but sudden storms*
> *are short;*
> *He tires betimes that spurs too fast betimes;*
> *With eager feeding food doth choke the feeder;*
> *Light vanity, insatiate cormorant,*
> *Consuming means, soon preys upon itself.*

This unkind, spiteful view of the cormorant came from the bird's proficiency as a fisher. While Western society was busy culling cormorants, who were viewed as competition for commercial anglers and fishing boats, other cultures embraced the bird and used it to their advantage. Cormorant fishing, which involves training cormorants to catch fish on a fisherman's behalf, seems to have been practised in many parts of the world, from Egypt to Peru, but was perfected in China and Japan at least a thousand years ago. Curiously, at the same time Shakespeare was staging *Richard II*, England's real monarch was starting to become rather fond of the cormorant. Possibly inspired by contemporary and exotic travel accounts of Asian cormorant fishing, King James VI decided he wanted his very own tame fishing bird. He employed his own 'Master of the Royal Cormorants', and set up cormorant houses near Westminster Palace, and even sent gifts of cormorants to other European royal families.

Stork

More than 6,000 years before Stonehenge was built, over in southeastern Turkey, a group of men and women were making their own glorious stone monument at Göbekli Tepe. They adorned its large, limestone pillars with pictures of animals important to them. Snakes, wild boar and foxes were all carved into stonework, but someone also took great care to chisel a particular species of bird: the stork.

This long-necked wading bird has long been praised for its ability to eat poisonous snakes and other reptiles. While we don't know why the people

of Göbekli Tepe felt compelled to honour the stork in stone, by the Greek era the bird was protected by law. Pliny the Elder, writing about the city of Thessaly, noted that 'So highly are they esteemed for their utility in destroying serpents [...] it was a capital crime for anyone to kill a stork.'

The belief about the goodness of the stork continued well into the eighteenth century. Charles Owen's 1742 *Natural History of Serpents* noted the stork's superior snake-killing abilities but also recorded an eccentric German folk belief. They are, he wrote, the 'Clergy's Friends' for they 'will not inhabit any City in Germany, where no Tythes are paid to the Priest.' A century earlier, English author Sir Thomas Browne had recorded an equally odd idea that storks only lived in 'Republics or free-states' and shied away from monarchies.

The stork was also thought to be a devoted family bird. Stork parents were considered exemplary, while grown chicks doted on their ageing mothers. Medieval monks rewrote, and reinforced, many of these beliefs. Thirteenth-century friar Thomas of Cantimpré, for instance, penned: 'Storks have the greatest affection for their young [...] the chicks have no less exceptional piety towards their mothers. For as much time as mothers spend in bringing up their young, so much time are they themselves nourished by the young.' In a sinister twist, a male stork was also said to kill its 'wife' if she was unfaithful. Roman author Claudius Aelianus noted that the stork was such a jealous bird it would even attack and blind a woman if she cheated on her husband.

Many northern European cultures encouraged the bird to live on their rooftops. In Dutch folklore, a stork settling on a home was a harbinger of family happiness, while in Hungary people placed old cartwheels on chimney tops to encourage storks to nest. The association of babies and storks probably drew on ancient ideas about the filial behaviour of storks but was firmly cemented in Hans Christian Andersen's *The Storks*. In this bizarre tale, the stork delivers babies to good parents with well-behaved children. Few know that the story also mentions that the stork brought dead babies to families with naughty siblings.

Sea Gull

Gentle sea gull, pray come here
Let me whisper in thine ear
Wilt thou fly a hundred miles
Where my sweet Maria smiles?

ANON (18TH CENTURY)

Sailors clearly had mixed feelings about the sea gull. For some, its appearance was a sign of optimism and good news, an indication that land, and by association home, wasn't too far away. Sea gulls, or 'sea-mews' as they were long known, were also employed as heraldic icons, as potent and recognizable symbols of hope. An absence of sea gulls, for mariners, also emphasized just how remote a location could be. Early twentieth-century Scottish-Canadian poet Robert William Service wrote a number of times about the bird – one poem in particular, *Stowaway*, drew on the connection between sea gulls and safety:

> *We'd left the sea-gulls long behind,*
> *And we were almost in mid-ocean;*
> *The sky was soft and blue and kind,*
> *The boat had scarcely any motion...*

The sea gull and its ties to the coastline also lent its name to a type of small boat: a sea-mew. Also called a yard tender, a sea-mew was a vessel used around shipyards to zip around and carry materials and people to larger moored vessels.

Sea gulls were sometimes thought, by superstitious sailors, to be the souls of departed colleagues, especially those who had drowned at sea. The sea gull's cries were also thought to warn a ship of bad weather. A now-unknown nineteenth-century unknown poet Roderick wrote:

> Go, listen to the wild sea mew, his home is the ocean wide
> He nestles on the billows, on the rising waves doth ride
> His scream is one of dread and fear, for the mariner knoweth well
> That the wild bird's cry, from sea to sky, doth sure a storm foretell.

One of the strangest practices relating to sea gulls was their use in early modern medicine. Royal College of Physicians doctor William Salmon, in his 1716 medical masterpiece *Pharmacopœia Londinensis*, recommended dried sea-mew brains for the 'falling-sickness' (epilepsy), either inhaled or taken internally with vinegar and honey. Sea gull heart was also prescribed to help with childbirth and 'the ashes of the whole bird' used as a diuretic.

Blue Jay

This elegant bird is distinguished as a sort of beau among the
feathered tenants of our woods by the brilliancy of his dress...

ALEXANDER WILSON (1854)

Blue jays, like many other corvids, are as bright as buttons. Recent work on avian cognition has shown jays to be exceptionally smart and curious, with researchers dubbing the bird 'feathered apes' for their superior intelligence. While modern experiments have established that jays are expert mimics, quick learners and opportunistic thieves, many indigenous American groups have long viewed the blue jay as a charismatic, morally ambivalent trickster. These two opposing sides of the jay's character – a bird viewed as both clever but also bold, mischievous and entertaining – represented something central about contradictions within the human condition. For the Tlingit people of the northwest coast of North America, the blue jay was known both as the 'camp robber', but also a helpful watchman, who could raise the alarm if danger approached. The Tlingit also admired the bird's cobalt plumage and chatty nature; in Tlingit mythology, the raven told the blue jay: 'You will have very fine clothes and be a good talker.'

Early Western attempts to describe the blue jay often blended admiration at the bird's pugnacity, and horror at its ability to attack fellow birds. Published in the middle of the eighteenth century, one journal – *The Western Miscellany* – described the blue jay as plucky enough to take on even an owl, especially with the help of its 'feathered fraternity'. Ganging together with his avian companions, a blue jay was said to intimidate birds of prey with all the fearless 'virulency of a Billingsgate mob', while crashing through the woodland, 'spreading alarm and sorrow all around him'. Other American literature also drew upon the idea of the blue jay as a problematic bird. In *To Kill a Mockingbird*,

siblings Jem and Scout are encouraged to single out one species of bird
for extermination – 'Shoot all the bluejays you want', their father tells them,
'if you can hit 'em' – an indication that blue jays were viewed as noisy idlers at
best, agents of the Devil at worst. In old southern folklore, the blue jay was said
to disappear every Friday to carry sticks to Satan, a belief that probably drew
from ancient European notions about corvids and the underworld (see Raven,
page 35).

The great American poet Emily Dickinson, however, seemed fond of the blue jay
and enjoyed the stoic resilience of the bird. She saw, perhaps, something of the
pioneer spirit in the blue jay, describing it as both 'neighbor and a warrior too':

> *The Pillow of this daring Head*
> *Is pungent Evergreens—*
> *His Larder—terse and Militant—*
> *Unknown—refreshing things—*
> *His character—a Tonic—*
> *His Future—a Dispute—*
> *Unfair an Immortality*
> *That leaves this Neighbor out.*

Duck

My sweetheart and I,
Sleepy face side by side,
Look out at the pond
Covered with snow and watch
The mandarin ducks floating.

TACHIBANA AKEMI (1812–68)

The duck was domesticated at least 4,000 years ago in southeast Asia and has, since then, lived in close proximity to humans. Many cultures have been drawn to ducks' behaviour and created both myths and tales inspired by many of the bird's traits, both real and perceived. In North American Indian mythology, for example, a figure called Shingebis occurs in several stories. A character who is often depicted as a duck, Shingebis is described as both plucky and resilient, an underdog who triumphs in harsh, wintry conditions when everyone else succumbs to the cold. In some North American tales, however, the duck is also gullible, easy prey. In the legend of the coyote and the ducks, a story told and retold across a number of different indigenous groups, a raft of ducks is tricked into being eaten by a hungry wild dog. Initially suspicious of the coyote, the ducks are only fooled into his lethal proximity by his endless flattery about their beautiful feathers.

All domestic ducks, apart from the muscovy, are descended from the wild mallard and different species have different characteristics. During the breeding season, many varieties of duck can become surprisingly sexually aggressive, a trait noted by medieval theologian Thomas of Cantimpré in the thirteenth century. Of ducks, he mused: 'Sometimes the males, where there are several together, are driven to such a frenzy of lust that they kill the only female duck by competing with each other'. This feverish mating behaviour didn't go unnoticed; in a number of countries, eating duck meat or duck eggs is still considered an aphrodisiac. In both the Philippines and Vietnam balut – a boiled egg that contains a duckling embryo – is believed to stir male sexual desire.

In ancient Egypt, duck iconography and sacrifice both seem linked to ideas about fertility and sexuality, although the exact meaning isn't clear, while in the Italian Renaissance, the health manual *Tacuinum Sanitatis* recommended cooking a meal of duck rubbed with oil to bolster someone feeling a little lacklustre.

In some countries, however, the duck represented fidelity and marriage, an idea tied to the belief that certain species mate for life. In China, for example, mandarin ducks are still much-loved icons of conjugal affection and marital longevity – well suited, happy couples are often compared to 'Two mandarin ducks playing in water'. In Korea, a pair of wooden mandarin ducks are often given as wedding gifts, or used as decoration in the ceremony, to represent faithful love and family. Similarly, in Japan, mandarin ducks are *oshidori*; auspicious symbols of enduring love.

Starling

...its varied song, its sprightly gestures, its glossy plumage, and, above all, its character as an insecticide—which last makes it the friend of the agriculturist and the grazier—render it an almost universal favourite.

ENCYCLOPÆDIA BRITANNICA (1911)

In 1702, French chemist Louis Lémery wrote a fascinating and highly readable book. Published under the title *Traité des aliments*, an English version was soon hot on its heels and had the lovely, rather long-winded title *A Treatise of All Sorts of Foods, Both Animal and Vegetable; also of Drinkables: Giving an Account how to chuse the best Sort of all Kinds*. It was a smorgasbord of delicious eighteenth-century ingredients and how to cook them. Among the familiar culinary favourites, a few notable surprises spring from the pages and give an insight into just how many wild birds we used to eat. From larks (see page 45) to moorhens, plovers (see page 86) to lapwings, almost nothing was considered taboo or too rare to hunt. And, of the starling, Lémery wrote 'Its Flesh is Nourishing, and yields good and solid Food, and is looked upon to be good for the Falling-sickness [epilepsy]'.

Lémery also added some interesting colour to his description of the starling. 'The Poets call it *Avis picturata*; because of its Beauty', he added with not a little admiration. According to the chemist, the starling was also to be 'found everywhere' – in summer it lives in the 'forests, watery places and meadows' but in winter shelters under the roofs of houses and 'many times get[s] into those Bottles which we fasten to the wall for the benefit of Sparrow' (see page 108).

Lémery was most impressed, however, by the starling's ability to form murmurations, those swirling, shapeshifting aerial swarms that 'fly with so much Force and Violence that they forme a kind of a Cloud, and make a sort of noise that might be taken for a Storm'. Pliny the Elder had spotted the phenomenon as early as the first century CE: 'It is a peculiarity of the starling to fly in troops, as it were, and then to wheel round in a globular mass like a ball, the central troop acting as a pivot for the rest', but it took another 1,500 years to give this spectacular display a name of its own. The word 'murmuration' means a grumbling or complaining sound and has been popular since at least Chaucer's time. Applied to starlings and their gatherings, however, it seems to have come into common use in the mid fifteenth-century 'A murmuracione of stares'. Few know that starlings were once simply called 'stares'. In fact, a stare was the name for an adult starling and a 'stærling' or 'sterlying' was its young.

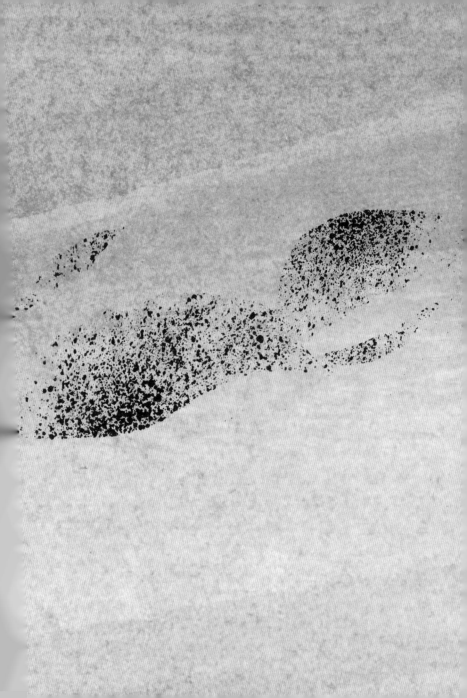

Swallow

The magicians think highly of [...] the small grits found in the crops of young swallows, tied to the left arm of the patient...

PLINY THE ELDER (1ST CENTURY CE)

If you've ever watched a swallow greedily devour flying insects on the wing, you'd be forgiven for thinking that's how it got its name. And yet the name 'swallow' has nothing to do with the bird's appetite. Its moniker probably comes from its distinctive forked tail. In Old English, the language of the Anglo-Saxons, the swallow was the *swealwe*, a word derived from the even-earlier proto-Germanic **swalwō*, a split stick or two-pronged fork.

The swallow is a summer visitor, its arrival a foretell of good weather. Both the Greeks and Romans had already noted the migratory patterns of this agile bird and coined a proverb we still use today – 'one swallow doesn't make a summer'. Its longer, original version goes something like this: 'It is not one swallow that brings in summer, just as it is not one quality that makes a good man. Swallows are a token of the beginning of summer, but one swallow is not a sure sign by itself. It is the same with all other things.'

In some European countries, 15 April was traditionally Swallow-Day, a celebration to mark the birds' arrival from Africa. According to the *Popular Educator*, a children's encyclopaedia from the nineteenth century:

'Everyone seems glad when the first swallow flits across the village green, but we sober English have never kept a "swallow holiday" on the 15th of April, which is in some parts of Europe, called "swallow day." In ancient Greece the children

might well clap their tiny hands
when the bird of spring appeared;
a holiday being then given to little boys
and girls. They danced in the marketplaces, wove
garlands of the early flowers, and shouted in the
luxury of childish joy.'

Swallows were such a beloved sign of summer that to harm one
was considered very bad luck. Rural superstition held that, if a
farmer killed a swallow or destroyed its nest, his harvest or milk
yield would be spoiled. You would also have to take care not to
disturb a nest: if a swallow built its home on your house, good
luck was ensured. If you deliberately damaged a swallow's
nest, however, financial failure would follow. To be 'swallow-
struck' was to be bewitched by a swallow, especially if it
landed on your shoulder. Or, if a swallow pecked a strand
of hair from your head – according to Irish custom – you
were destined for purgatory.

Swallows, like many species of bird, often ingest small
stones to help digestion. Classical physicians were
fascinated with these tiny pebbles that, if taken from a
dead swallow, were thought to cure blindness. Pliny the
Elder wrote that swallows intentionally consumed these
'swallow-stones' to heal their own eyes and improve the sight
of their chicks. By wearing these tiny amulets against the skin,
patients hoped their own eyesight might too be restored.

Kestrel

I caught this morning morning's minion, king-
dom of daylight's dauphin, dapple-dawn-drawn Falcon, in his riding
Of the rolling level underneath him steady air, and striding
High there, how he rung upon the rein of a wimpling wing...

GERARD MANLEY HOPKINS (1877)

Gerard Manley Hopkins said, of his poem *The Windhover*, that it was probably his finest work. The poem is not only a sublime description of a 'windhover', or common kestrel, as it twists, turns and hangs in the air, but is also a deeply personal meditation on God, faith and the raw beauty of Nature.

The kestrel was also an unusual bird for Manley Hopkins to have chosen. In the eighteenth and nineteenth centuries, many birds of prey were either quarry to be mounted in a glass cage, or the gamekeeper's enemy. In Tudor times, the kestrel was also viewed as the lowliest of the predatory birds, but for a different reason. In medieval times, everyone who could afford to keep a 'hawking' bird did. Although different species were often used for different kinds of hunting, birds were rigorously tied to the feudal system and wealth. As laid out in a fifteenth-century manuscript, 'Harleian MS20', the rules were clear:

An Eagle for an Emperor,
a Gyrfalcon for a King;
a Peregrine for a Prince,
a Saker for a Knight,
a Merlin for a Lady;
a Goshawk for a Yeoman,
a Sparrowhawk for a Priest,
a Musket for a Holy water Clerk,
a Kestrel for a Knave.

A kestrel, 'a hawk of base, unserviceable breed', belonged to the knave, a boy or servant, but was also a medieval nickname for someone without scruples. The kestrel, therefore, signified the dishonest man, as Edmund Spenser alluded to in *The Faerie Queene*, published in 1590:

> *Ne thought of honour euer did assay*
> *His baser brest, but in his kestrell kind*
> *A pleasing vaine of glory vaine did find...*

Shakespeare also used the kestrel, a bird he calls a 'staniel', in a scene about trickery. In *Twelfth Night*, a forged letter is deliberately left for Malvolio to find. Fabian and Toby joke to each other about Malvolio's credulity as he hovers over the words:

> *FABIAN: What dish o' poison has she dressed him!*
> *TOBY: And with what wing the staniel checks at it!*

The association between the kestrel and the knave may even explain the bird's name. Many etymologies link the modern word 'kestrel' to the French *crecerelle*, which means 'rattle' and may refer to the bird's distinguishing call. But another possibility is that kestrel may come from *coystrel* or *coystril*, a long-forgotten medieval word for a servant or boy who carried a knight's arms. It seems the kestrel may truly belong to the knave after all.

Parrot

Our parrot, sent from India's farthest shore,
Our parrot, prince of mimics, is no more.
Throng to his burial, pious tribes of air,
With rigid claw your tender faces tear!

OVID (43 BCE–18 CE)

It's tantalizing to imagine that the West had never seen a parrot until explorers in the fifteenth and sixteenth centuries brought incredible birds back from their global plundering. And yet, the parrot has been an exotic pet in Europe for at least 2,000 years.

Ctesias was a Greek physician with a vivid imagination. Many of the tales from his travels around the Persian Empire, at the end of the fifth century BCE, stretch credulity but not all his descriptions are entirely fictitious. As resident doctor at the Persian Court in southwestern Asia, Ctesias saw many exciting and rare treasures traded from India and beyond. One particular prize, a beautiful bird from the Indian subcontinent, he described as the size of a hawk with a dark crimson face. It also had, he noted, a black beard, blue neck and shoulders the colour of red cinnabar, a pigment used for dying. Thanks to the detective work of later scholars, we now think that Ctesias was gazing with wonder at a male plum-headed parakeet. This is probably the earliest description of a member of the parrot family in the Western world.

The parrot could apparently talk and 'converse like a human in Indian but if taught Greek, it can also speak', a talent that has led to many famous people owning parrots down the centuries. Ovid, the first century BCE Roman poet, famously composed an elegy to his mistress' dead parrot. 'Yet still from failing throat thy accents rung; Farewell, Corinna! cried thy dying tongue', penned Ovid, a melodramatic and probably completely made-up account of the parrot's last words. In the thirteenth century, Holy Roman Emperor Frederick II had in his extensive menagerie an Australasian cockatoo gifted by an Egyptian sultan. And, back in England, Henry VIII was particularly fond of his African grey parrot, a bird that even had a satirical work written for him by poet John Skelton called *Speke, Parrot*.

The royal connection with parrots continued. The Duchess of Richmond and Lennox and her African grey parrot were apparently so firmly wedded that when the duchess died, the parrot also metaphorically fell off its perch in grief. The bird was hastily stuffed and displayed in Westminster Abbey, and is believed to be the world's oldest, if rather badly, taxidermied bird. And, in the nineteenth century, Queen Victoria owned at least three parrots during her lifetime: Lory, her childhood Loriini parrot; a Brazilian parrot called Pedro; and Coco, an African grey, which was taught to speak French, make jokes and even chant 'God save the Queen'.

Partridge

*Our forest air has not disagreed with her; you'll find her all plump as a
partridge. How Sir Walter came by her, that you most learn; but he has
always been a devil of a fellow, from his youth, for fighting and wenching.*

SIR HENRY BATE DUDLEY (1791)

There can surely be no other bird that is named after a fart. The word 'partridge'
comes from the Old French *pertis* which, if you trace its origins back to ancient
Greek, comes from the verb *perdesthai* – to break wind. An unfortunate name
for an exquisite little bird perhaps but, if you've ever heard a partridge launch
itself, wings flapping furiously, you can see where ancient ornithologists were
coming from.

The partridge has, in fact, been curiously linked to other bodily functions.
It was a bird thought to have a voracious sexual appetite, one that was so
powerful it would try to mate with almost anything. Aristotle, writing in the
fourth century BCE, maintained that the male partridge had intercourse with its
own chicks as soon as they hatched, while four centuries later Pliny the Elder
wrote that partridges experienced such violent lust they even tried to mate
with the heads of fowlers who were hunting them. This strange and prurient
speculation only continued throughout the ages, with the male partridge
accused of destroying its own eggs so a female wouldn't be too busy to have
time for mating, and having such a 'strong liking of lechery [they] forgetteth
the sexe and distinction of male and female'.

Given the partridges' alleged insatiable appetite, it's perhaps no surprise that many physicians viewed the partridge as an ingredient for a love potion. One Babylonian text from 800 BCE prescribed a partridge's fresh heart and blood for lack of libido. The *Cyranides*, a fourth-century compilation of magic and medicine, recommended partridge eggs to incite lust. The *Cyranides* also endorsed partridge shells, crushed and mixed with wax and zinc oxide, to give droopy breasts a welcome plumping boost. And, in Nicholas Culpeper's 1651 *A Directory of Midwives*, he suggested that:

'Whatsoever any Creature is addicted extreamly to, they move the man that eats them, to the like by their Mummial vertue; therefore Partridges; Quails, Sparrows, &c. being exceeding addicted to Venery [sexual pleasure], they work the same in those men and women that eat them.'

By Victorian times, to be described as 'plump as a partridge' was a compliment, albeit one with comely, often sexualized undertones. In *Martin Chuzzlewit*, Charles Dickens wrote: 'Plump as any partridge was each Miss Mould, and Mrs M. was plumper than the two together', while in *A Streetcar Named Desire*, Tennessee Williams' 1947 play, Blanche gives her youngster sister Stella a backhanded compliment: 'But you— you've put on some weight, yes, you're just as plump as a little partridge! And it's so becoming to you!'

Eagle

A lover's eyes will gaze an eagle blind...

WILLIAM SHAKESPEARE (1598)

On a balmy summer's evening in 1958, an Orkney farmer uncovered an astonishing tomb. He'd stumbled upon a small stone chamber filled with human remains. Alongside the skulls and skeletons of over 320 people, archaeologists later discovered the talons and bones from as many as 20 sea eagles. The tomb, now dubbed the 'Tomb of the Eagles', was first built around 5,000 years ago. The eagles' remains, however, were placed inside nearly a thousand years later. Any burial site is special for the surviving relatives but to have such a long-standing, repeatedly visited place of remembrance is deeply moving. Archaeologists also suspect that the eagles' claws and bones formed part an important ancestral ritual.

Many cultures have associated the eagle with death, rebirth and the heavens. One Babylonian myth talked about a ruler who reigned for over 1,500 years. King Etana, however, was struggling to sire a son until an eagle took him into the sky to find the plant of fertility and birth. Roman texts revealed the practice of releasing eagles at emperors' funerals. Pyres were lit, with a caged eagle inside, and the bird would be released to symbolize the ruler's flight to heaven. In Christianity, too, the eagle represented Christ's ascension, but also the feeling of soaring, strengthening spirituality. Isaiah 40:31, for example, promised: 'they who wait for the Lord shall renew their strength; they shall mount up with wings like eagles'.

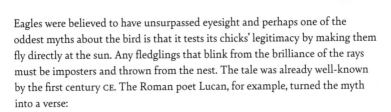

In the mythologies of multiple ancient cultures, the sun is depicted as a bird. And for many, that bird is an eagle. The eagle's supreme ability to reach dizzying heights, and seemingly track across the sky like the moving sun, encouraged early civilizations to depict their sun gods as eagles, or have an eagle companion. The spirit animal of the Aztec sun god Huitzilopochtli (see page 88) was the eagle, while across many Near Eastern cultures – from Egypt to Mesopotamia – the eagle-winged sun was a symbol often associated with power, divinity and monarchy.

Eagles were believed to have unsurpassed eyesight and perhaps one of the oddest myths about the bird is that it tests its chicks' legitimacy by making them fly directly at the sun. Any fledglings that blink from the brilliance of the rays must be imposters and thrown from the nest. The tale was already well-known by the first century CE. The Roman poet Lucan, for example, turned the myth into a verse:

> *So the bird of Jove*
> *Turns his new fledglings to the rising sun*
> *And such as gaze upon the beams of day*
> *With eyes unwavering, for the use of heaven*
> *He rears; but such as blink at Phoebus' rays*
> *Casts from the nest.*

Fifteen hundred years later, Shakespeare was still alluding to the strange story of the eagle's paternity test. In *Henry VI*, Richard asks 'Nay, if thou be that princely eagle's bird, Show thy descent by gazing 'gainst the sun.'

ACKNOWLEDGEMENTS

What a pleasure it is to work with such a fantastic bunch of people. Harriet, Stacey, Claire and Clover – you are my complete dream team and lovely, lovely women to boot. Making books is a collaborative process – I'm so lucky to work with individuals who have great editorial judgement, fantastic ideas and an unwaveringly good sense of design. Thank you for making this such a gorgeous book.

Quadrille, Penguin Random House UK, One
Embassy Gardens, 8 Viaduct Gardens, London
SW11 7BW

Quadrille Publishing Limited is part of the Penguin
Random House group of companies whose addresses
can be found at global.penguinrandomhouse.com

Penguin
Random House
UK

Published by Quadrille in 2025

www.penguin.co.uk

A CIP catalogue record for this book is
available from the British Library

ISBN 978 1 837 833 061

10 9 8 7 6 5 4 3 2 1

Managing Director Sarah Lavelle
Editorial Director Harriet Butt
Designer Alicia House
Illustrator Clover Robin
Production Director Stephen Lang
Production Manager Sabeena Atchia

Colour reproduction by F1

Printed in China by C&C Offset Printing Co., Ltd.

The authorised representative in the EEA is
Penguin Random House Ireland, Morrison
Chambers, 32 Nassau Street, Dublin D02 YH68.

Penguin Random House is committed to a
sustainable future for our business, our readers
and our planet. This book is made from Forest
Stewardship Council® certified paper.

MIX
Paper | Supporting
responsible forestry
FSC® C018179
www.fsc.org